D1227094

The Smallest Grand Opera in the World

Table of Contents

The Smallest Grand Opera in the World

By

Anthony (Tony) Amato

with Rochelle Mancini

iUniverse, Inc.
Bloomington

The Smallest Grand Opera in the World

iUniverse books may be ordered through booksellers, at www.amato.org, or by contacting:

iUniverse
1663 Liberty Drive
Bloomington, IN 47403
www.iuniverse.com
1-800-Authors (1-800-288-4677)

Because of the dynamic nature of the Internet, any web addresses or links contained in this book may have changed since publication and may no longer be valid. The views expressed in this work are solely those of the author and do not necessarily reflect the views of the publisher, and the publisher hereby disclaims any responsibility for them.

ISBN: 978-1-4620-1049-3 (sc)
ISBN: 978-1-4620-1048-6 (hc)
ISBN: 978-1-4502-9917-6 (e)

Printed in the United States of America
iUniverse rev. date: 08/10/2011

"The irrepressible and irreplaceable Tony Amato taught a generation of opera singers their craft with expertise, humor, and love. I will cherish and be forever grateful that I was one of those lucky ones."

–Mignon Dunn, Metropolitan Opera

"Anthony Amato and his late wife Sally became 20th-century legends in the opera realm of New York City. Their love of the art form gave birth to an opera company designed to provide fledgling performers like myself both a training ground and an opportunity to make their New York City debuts. . . . Singers of the caliber of Mignon Dunn, Chester Ludgin, Jon Frederick West, and Walter McNeil, to name but a few, learned and grew under the loving tutelage of the Amatos, and went on to number amongst some of the world's most respected operatic artists. I am sure I mirror the sentiments of all thus favored when, on the occasion of the publication of Tony's memoirs, I, from the depths of my heart, say 'Sia benedetto, Tony e Sally; io vi ringrazia mille volte con saluti cari e un abbraccio!'"

–George Shirley, Metropolitan Opera
The J. Edgar Maddy Distinguished University
Emeritus Professor of Music (Voice)
University of Michigan School of Music, Theatre, & Dance

Introduction

F OR a number of years, people have been telling me that I should write about the Amato Opera and the life my wife Sally and I made for ourselves out of nothing much more than dreams at first. I didn't take the suggestion very seriously while I was in the midst of a grueling production schedule that didn't leave much time to reflect on my life. Since the Bowery Theatre—the Smallest Grand Opera in the World—closed its doors in May, 2009, my life has by no means been slow and peaceful, but it has given me the opportunity to think back over the whole span of my career, and it has brought such wonderful memories that I decided that I would like to share them with others.

I think the most important thing I've always wanted to tell struggling artists is that if an immigrant from a small town in Italy with a limited education like me could make a success of building an opera company, then they too can fulfill their aspirations!

It's not just our technical knowledge that makes us what we are to become. My experiences as a human being before my music career began were the basis of all my future success.

I learned from my family, as they struggled to make a new life for themselves in the United States. I learned from my idealistic father (who read Dante and Shakespeare—in Italian—in his rare spare time) that, if you tried as hard as possible and didn't give in to discouragement, you could make progress and eventually attain your goals. Against the odds—and perhaps against all reason—he believed that he could bring his sons from Italy to this country and that they could follow their dreams and become successful musicians. And he was right! Without music degrees or advanced education, we all supported our families and fulfilled our musical aspirations.

As for me, my drive to succeed started very early in life, back in my teenage years as a short-order cook and a butcher in New Haven. Looking back on it, I believe that one of my greatest assets was that I had a knack of listening and observing—whether it was learning how to butcher a cow or figuring out what it was that a conductor did up there on the podium. I stored away everything I learned, always with the thought that "I might need that sometime," no matter what the subject was.

It definitely helped my musical career that I was a natural showman and that, even as a child of 10, I sang for friends and family and accompanied my older brothers on "gigs" with dance bands and other orchestras. Once I got in front of the public, I couldn't stop gathering more and more knowledge, whether it was how the conductor got the musicians to follow his lead, or how the suave dance band singer captured the attention of his audience, or why people laughed if you waited an extra beat before delivering the punchline. If you are a "pack rat" for information, I don't believe anything can get in the way of personal progress. With this habit of taking in information (some might call it 'stealing'), I found the means of searching out what I needed to know before taking the next step forward.

Deep down, I've always faced my art with great humility. I understand what a gift it is to work in the field of opera. I am filled with gratitude that I've been given the privilege of working in what I love best, and I never had the slightest urge to impress people with my knowledge. There's a big distinction between being a showman and a show-off. Opera is there for all of us to make use of and to love.

What are some of the things I have learned? Well, for one, while education and degrees from universities and conservatories certainly can help with introductions into more exalted music circles, I am not sorry about the course of my own life. If I had had the opportunity to gain advanced education, my life would most probably have gone in another direction. I most likely would have had a bigger singing career, but I never would have had the opportunity to develop the Amato Opera as a place for young people to gain precisely the experience they weren't usually getting in the university and conservatory system. Because I struggled so hard to gain the information I needed and was keenly aware of what I *didn't* know, I wanted to make it easier for others starting out upon their music careers. Looking back, maybe that wasn't the easiest way to make use of my life's lessons. But it certainly was fulfilling!

I don't have any illusions about what it takes to run an opera company. And there is no doubt that it is a more difficult undertaking today in the 21st century than it was in the heady, post-war days of the late 1940s, when returning soldiers and new entrepreneurs thought they could do anything they set their minds on.

But there is one thing I wouldn't change about advising anyone with energy and a dream: Do It Yourself! Don't spend your time looking for angels and sponsors. While it is nice to have support and backing—monetary and inspirational—there is no substitute for rolling up your sleeves and getting the job done. Now that the Amato Opera is no longer performing, a few of my former students have tried to continue, but I hope this memoir will encourage many more to try. The more the better! The more the exposure to opera the better!

Of course, one person can't do everything and there will always be regrets. Personally, I regret that I didn't work harder to become a good pianist, but my schedule never allowed the time. How it would have helped, though, especially since our budget never made it possible to have orchestra rehearsals. But maybe that made me a better conductor, as I had to strive harder to express myself through the tools I *did* have at my command when communicating my ideas under time constraints to my musicians and singers.

I was lucky that I never had trouble conveying what I wanted from my artists through my voice, whether singing or speaking. I never worried about "saving my voice," whether in rehearsals or in performance. I credit this at least in part to good genes. You should have heard my mother's fine and powerful voice when she found me doing something I shouldn't have been doing!—even though I only caught her singing in secret when she thought she was alone.

I repeat it again: Do It Yourself! And I add one more step: Learn to Know Yourself! Young people need to sift the information they get, apply what works for them, and then, finally, know when to stop taking advice from others. Take everything teachers and colleagues have to give, but learn your own limitations well enough to make your own judgments about what is right for you. Maybe that sums up what my goal was for the Amato Opera. I wanted to give young artists the opportunity—singing and performing under supportive direction—to discover their own personal paths, whether as professional singers, performers in church choirs, conductors and directors, or teachers. Only by stretching their limits in such a performance setting can people learn their proper paths.

I have always believed that this was one of my most important goals: helping people find their true callings in the world of music. There is room for all of us, and everyone who knocks at the door should be embraced and made welcome.

I have enjoyed telling my story in these pages. It has given me an opportunity to express my thanks to the many, many people who have made my success possible. The one torment is the fear that I will inadvertently forget to mention people in the pages that follow. But, now, it is my pleasure to invite readers into *The Smallest Grand Opera in the World* to meet the literally thousands of people who have been a part of the Amato Opera. And if what follows brings a song or a favorite aria to mind, then so much the better!

Anthony (Tony) Amato—July 2010

Part I - The Early Days

I WAS born on July 21, 1920 in the small Italian seaside town of Minori, then a community of about 2,000 people on the Amalfi Drive south of Naples, in the province of Salerno. Before I was born, my father Antonio had been drafted into the army during World War I, in spite of being head of both a family and a local pasta-producing business employing about 25 local women. Being an ardent pacifist, he managed through guile and intelligence to stay away from the battlefield. His younger brother Ciccio was less fortunate and was severely wounded at the infamous battle of Caporetto. While away at war, the family business was entrusted to his younger brother Alfonso, who avoided conscription by becoming a local customs officer. He succeeded in running the business

An old postcard view of Minori: my house was behind the corner, at the left of this photo.

into the ground, subsequently absconding with whatever money was left.

After returning to Minori at the end of the war, my father almost died during the worldwide flu epidemic of 1918. He managed to survive, but economic conditions kept worsening and, in 1923, he decided to go to America to see if life would be better for us there.

During that year in the U.S., since he was making a decent living, he came to the conclusion that the country offered opportunities for his musician sons to achieve great success, so he made the decision to bring the rest of the family to America. So, in 1924, my father returned to Italy to take us all to a new life in the United States. But on the morning of our departure for the 'Promised Land,' our 17-year-old sister Carmelina was nowhere to be found. She had eloped with her boyfriend. My mother insisted that she would not leave Italy until she knew the whereabouts of her daughter. So, that same day, with the tickets already bought, Papa departed once more for America, taking with him only my oldest brother Salvatore, who was already a highly-talented flutist, and leaving behind Mother with the four youngest of us boys, as well as our missing sister Carmelina, who soon reappeared with her new husband Ciccio, a tailor.

The next three years in Italy were fun, especially during the summers, which we spent mostly on the beach and attending the various religious festivals of our nearby towns—Amalfi, Atrani, Maiori, Ravello. These coastal towns were popular during the summer months, with each one competing for the largest number of the foreign tourists who came to our region attracted by the natural beauty of the beaches and picturesque mountains with orange and lemon trees in full bloom. Because Minori was only a 10-minute walk from the very popular tourist destination of Amalfi, which attracted a huge summer crowd of mostly Germans and Scandinavians, we got the overflow when the Amalfi hotels were full and Minori had quite a few tourists in the summer months.

Each township worked overtime trying to outdo the other in honoring their own particular patron saint, and there were plenty of fireworks, with famous symphony bands invited for the evening's entertainment. Our town, Minori, had a local band in which my father, an ardent music lover, had participated in his earlier days as principle trombone and baritone player, giving him the opportunity and enjoyment of performing major arias from mostly Verdi operas. My older brothers Alfonse and Nadir started their musical studies with the same local bandmaster, Matteo.

My brother Alberto and I were inseparable during this period and never missed the local festivals. Particularly memorable was the feast of Saint Pantaleone in Ravello, an extraordinarily beautiful and historic town on the hilltop above Minori. My father never failed

to mention how Ravello had been visited by such great composers as Richard Wagner and Richard Strauss. It was also a favorite vacation spot for Leopold Stokowski and Greta Garbo. And Gore Vidal resided for many years at the famed Villa Ciambrone, where major European orchestras would come annually for

(l. to r.) My brother Alberto, Ciccio, and me on the beach in Minori. As usual, I am laughing.

concerts in the villa's magnificent gardens.

Getting to Ravello for non-vehicle owners meant traversing a steep path through the hillside, which included crossing the local

cemetery. This adventure took the better part of an hour. The return trip, when darkness set in, took much less time, what with Alberto and me setting speed records as we crossed the cemetery, trying to avoid being caught by the evil ghosts.

There were also interesting holiday rituals that intrigued us children. I particularly remember how Mother, during the Easter holidays, would bathe our feet with flower petals immersed in water, keeping with the tradition of Christ bathing the feet of the Apostles.

(l. to r.) Alberto, Alfonse, and me in our "boy scout" uniforms.

Other favorite family times were spent on the mountaintop of St. Nicola Villamena, where Mama had property that she had inherited from her foster parents. We would have picnics there on sunny days, surrounded by fragrant lemon trees. Our drinking cups at these picnics would be the lemons themselves, which Mama would cut in half and scrape out before filling them with fresh water or wine.

Another memory of my childhood is how Alberto and I would

climb up to the roof of our house in Minori. Next door to us was a hotel (*albergo*) with a huge fig tree that grew up to the level of our own rooftop. We would take a long fork and spear "stolen" figs from this tree for a particularly luscious breakfast. Other times (since we were always up for a snack), my mother would send a basket down a rope to us where we were playing on the street. Inside we would find bread deliciously slathered with olive oil.

By 1927, my father, now a U.S. citizen, sent for the family left behind in Italy to join him (Mama, Nadir, Alfonse, Alberto, and me), leaving only our sister Carmelina and her husband in the family home in Minori. According to Italian immigration laws, my sister couldn't join us, because she was now considered part of her husband's family and no longer legally a part of ours. All four of us boys were very excited and looked forward to the trip—but not my mother, who dreaded the ocean voyage of 11 days and the anticipated seasickness.

My last night in Minori was a magical one for me. I secretly met my sweetheart after dark and we hid under the bow of a boat right on the beach. I distinctly remember giving her a goodbye kiss. We were the same age—all of seven years old!

The first three days through the Mediterranean on the luxury ship *Conte Biancamano* were a joy. Our second-class accommodations included our own separate dining table, the opportunity to watch passengers

Our house (r.) in Minori next to the albergo. Alas, the fig tree cannot be seen.

gambling in the casino, and allowed us to participate in various other activities. On the third night of our trip, the ship went through the Straits of Gibraltar and entered the Atlantic—and that was when our troubles began. The oldest of the four boys, Nadir, then 17 years old, had been put in charge, but unfortunately was the first to succumb to the waves of the Atlantic. My mother Maria soon followed, then Alfonse, leaving my ten-year-old brother Alberto and me as the only able-bodied men to leave our cabin. For the next seven days, we had the run of the ship.

By the last morning of our trip, the rest of the family had reasonably recovered and were able to come on deck to enjoy our entrance into the New York harbor, where we arrived at daybreak. We marveled at the imposing Statue of Liberty and the mob waiting at dockside, not to mention the excitement when Mama spotted our father and pointed him out to us where he was waiting for us on shore.

Papa and some *paesans* living in Manhattan met us at the docking of the ship and we spent our first night in America at our friends' house in Mount Vernon, where we were treated royally. The next day, we left for New Haven, Connecticut, where many of our *paesans* had settled down. Papa and Salvatore had an apartment ready for us on Greene Street, with all the modern facilities we didn't have in Minori, particularly central heating and an incinerator in the hallway! For income, Papa had a small candy store. Since his first week in America, Salvatore had been employed as a musician. From the very beginning, he toured across the country, playing in movie houses, where a live orchestra served to accompany the silent films of the day.

I attended grammar school at Columbus School. "O'Talian"—that's what they called me in the schoolyard, but I don't recall if I ever struggled learning the English language. I looked forward to reading aloud in the classroom. I guess the ham in me showed up at an early age. "Me, Myself, and I" was my favorite poem. Baseball quickly became my favorite sport. I had great fun with my schoolmates when I formed an all-star Italian team with famous players of that era: DiMaggio, Lazzeri, Bonura, Cuccinelli, Crosseti, Camilli. I ran into a problem when I was looking for a third Italian outfielder. I solved the problem by choosing a star outfielder, Richard Hall, and conveniently making him an Italian, translating his name to Riccardo Corridoro. That completed my all-Italian all-star team!

In 1930, Papa went into a new business venture: he opened a small pool parlor with card tables on Wooster Street in New Haven, where the local Italians played their favorite card games, *scopa* and *zichinetti*. After school, my duties were selling cigarettes and candies and setting up the pool balls for the next game.

Next, Papa, always thinking big, acquired a classy family restaurant in a well-to-do part of New Haven. This venture turned into a financial disaster. Papa was a very proud man and abhorred the idea that any of his children should support his family, so he was always searching for new ventures in hopes of success. In the next year or two, Papa acquired a diner, The Silver Lunch, located at the local farmer's market, in a commercial and dangerous section of town known for break-ins and thefts. Because he had to be up by 4 AM to prepare for the morning customers, Papa had to sleep in the rear room of the diner—with a gun under his pillow for protection. On many 'no school' days, I slept next to him. Was I scared? You bet I was!

The diner was open from 5 A.M. until late in the evening. Alberto (now diligently studying piano) and I were chosen to help after school hours, serving sandwiches and coffee at the counter. Even though I was only about 13 years old, my duties included being a short-order cook and chasing after customers who forgot (accidentally on purpose) to pay their bills. I always remember how, once, when the cook was late, in order not to lose a sale, I cooked my first lobster. To my surprise, the patron complimented me on it! The Silver Lunch provided a decent livelihood for the family for many years.

By the age of 12, my infatuation with singing had already begun. In looking back and thinking about how my brothers and I were all so in love with music and how most of us ended up making a living in the field of music—something quite rare for a family of new immigrants—I would say that my father was responsible. I think about how unusual it was that he had originally come to the United States to investigate the possibilities for his musician sons, and how he sent for us when he felt that he had found a country that would nurture our musical ambitions.

He himself loved opera. His favorite opera was *Ballo in Maschera* and he never tired of telling us about hearing the incomparable baritone, Riccardo Stracciari, in the role of Renato. He often hummed the aria "Eri Tu," which he knew very well, having played it on his baritone horn in the local town band before he came to the United States. My father's interest in the arts was unlimited, as was his love of poetry.

One of the fondest memories I have as a child in New Haven was our RCA victrola and the record our uncle, Angelo Pappalardo, himself a non-musician, gave us of Titta Ruffo singing the "Credo" from Verdi's *Otello*. On the opposite side was a recording of the great second act duet, "Si pel ciel," from the same opera. My brother Alberto and I agree, to this day, that this performance has never been equaled.

When I was very young, I saw the 1929 movie, *The Pagan*,

about an opera singer, starring the movie idol of the day, Ramon Novarro, playing the betrayed husband and clown and singing the aria "Vesti la Giubba" from Leoncavallo's opera *I Pagliacci*. From then on, there was no stopping me, and whenever there was a family occasion, I was called on to sing the aria.

By the early '30s, at the height of the Depression, marathon dancing became all the rage. My brothers Salvatore, Nadir, and Alfonse were part of a dance orchestra and I would often join them to sing my celebrated aria about a despairing clown, completely out of keeping with the rest of the music, which consisted of the popular tunes of the day, while the exhausted couples tried to keep dancing so they wouldn't be eliminated from the competition. I remember once that one of the dance participants was a handsome young man named Frank LoVecchio, later to become the famous Frankie Laine, who was to immortalize the song "Mule Train."

Alberto (who, as the only pianist in the family, ended up accompanying all of us) and I also performed at other special events, such as weddings and local festivals, where I would sing Neapolitan songs and popular operatic arias like Arlecchino's serenade from *I Pagliacci*.

In 1935, I graduated from Columbus grammar school. Because of financial and family problems, Papa's future plans for me and Alberto turned into unexpected directions. Our sister Carmelina in Italy, now with two children, Trofimena and Nicola, became fatally ill with peritonitis. Mother made a hurried trip to Italy to care for her before her demise in 1938.

Alberto was now an honor high school graduate and an accomplished pianist, with family expectations that he would attend a conservatory in Italy to continue his studies as a conductor. But, because of the family's financial straits during the Depression, Papa's future musical plans for Alberto were cancelled. Discouraged and disappointed, Alberto accepted Papa's decision that he become a druggist, and he enrolled in the local pharmacy college. He had to discontinue his piano studies, but always returned whenever possible to his beloved Mozart and Beethoven sonatas, so he remained a fine pianist. For all of us, there was no change in the family's favorite topic of conversation. Whenever we gathered together, the subject was always music, from performance to discussions about the latest operatic superstar or new conducting phenomenon.

As for my future, since I was always efficient in Papa's business ventures, it was decided that I would attend commercial high school. My high school days lasted only one-and-a-half years, but they were the most fun time of my youth. I didn't do much homework, but somehow I was quite good in the classroom. I especially enjoyed my civics class, taught by Mr. Valenti, where we dicussed the current news. In our debates, Mussolini was usually the favorite topic. Mr. Valenti also happened to be the coach of the school's fencing team. At his suggestion, I tried out for the team and chose the foil as my weapon over the epée and sabre. Foil requires speed and technique, while the sabre and epée are better suited for tall, brawny fencers. As a freshman, I made the team with my speed and tricky maneuvers. I thought I was quite good, until our team was invited to compete against the Army plebes at West Point. I lost all my bouts. Nevertheless, it was a great day to remember. The cadets showed us about the grounds, and we joined them for lunch in the mess hall.

During my high school days, I became close friends with a neighbor, Armando Antonio De Vivo. We all called him Chic. He was a novice in opera, but he loved to sing (tenor) and was a great whistler, which often got him into trouble when his avid whistling was misinterpreted by passing beautiful girls. Chic and I were inseparable in playing ball and practicing our fencing. He was always there when I needed assistance with my family work duties. I treasure his friendship forever.

With family problems still mounting, Papa decided that I should become a butcher. It never even occurred to me to object to my father's ruling, which was made without consulting me. In an Italian household, the father's word was law. So, at the age of 16, I dropped out of high school, even though all my teachers begged me not to. Within a six-month period, in the local meat establishment, I learned the butcher's trade completely, from skinning calves to preparing meat for the counter displays.

In 1936, Tony's Meat Market opened on Grand Avenue, a commercial working-class section of New Haven. My responsibilities were to serve and run the meat department.

We soon expanded by adding groceries, fruits, and vegetables. That was Papa's job—to go to the farmer's market early in the morn-

Though I don't have a photo of Tony's Meat Market, this photo reminds me very much of our shop, with the hinds of beef hanging from the ceiling on hooks. (c)

ing to do the buying. Many times, Papa went overboard when he saw a bargain. He once bought 40 sacks of potatoes, even though our average sales were never more than two sacks a week. The potatoes soon spoiled and all had to be dumped.

At first, business was so bad that often I'd retrieve used shopping bags, press and fold them by hand, and reuse them for the next sale. That's being thrifty—or, as we Italians say it, *miserabile*. Even-

Mama and Papa Amato

tually, we built a steady following of customers. I gained the reputation of being the best local veal cutlet cutter in town, which wasn't easy. The Italians like their veal cutlets cut paper-thin.

Papa's manner with the clientele didn't make him too popular. He always scolded the customers if they examined and touched the produce before buying. The result was that whenever he was seen in the store, the customers would shop elsewhere, forcing me, in a diplomatic way, to send him home to "rest." At home, his complaint to Mama was always: "That son of yours threw me out again!"

It was about this time that the singing bug really hit me. I began taking voice lessons from Professor F. Riggio, a maestro from Palermo, Sicily and also a close friend of the family. All my brothers studied under his tutelage. Maestro Riggio produced and conducted yearly opera productions, featuring Metropolitan Opera artists, at the Shubert Theatre in New Haven. Being his favorite pupil, he would cast me in the comprimario (secondary) roles, such as Goro, Beppe, Arturo, and Trabucco. I began to dream of myself as the 'local boy who makes it big!'

My daily routine would be: work at the butcher shop from 8 A.M to 6 P.M.; rush home three city blocks away on Olive Street; Mother would have my supper ready; wash up; then rush off 8-10 blocks to the studio uptown for my singing and coaching lessons with Professor Riggio.

At home there was always the sound of music, with my brothers all practicing their musical instruments. Our Sunday dinners, at my father's insistence, always turned into a family musicale, with all my brothers participating. This motivated me to concentrate on my solfeggio, harmony, and theory, and I studied a bit of piano and trumpet, all with the assistance of my brothers. Not knowing it at the time, my study of solfeggio was giving me exactly what I needed to lay the groundwork for my future work.

In the course of the first two years (1937-38) in the butcher shop, lifting huge hinds of beef in and out of a large Frigidaire freezer caught up with me physically. I became very ill and, in 1938, within a period of six months, I had to undergo two operations, with two weeks of recuperation in between. It was during this period that I was called up for induction into army duty. The doctors looked at my physical records and quickly sent me home. I was 4F.

While I was recuperating, during my absence in the store, Papa was left in complete charge. The result was that the customers stopped shopping with us. This forced me to cut short my recuperation time and rush back to the store, bringing the business back to normal.

For the next two years, the responsibilities at the store became even more strenuous; however, my opera studies and occasional performing with famous opera stars under Maestro Riggio's leadership somehow made the time pass quickly. I remember how self-conscious I was back then about my 5'3" height, and when I was asked to sing the role of the bridegroom, Arturo, in *Lucia di Lammermoor*, I bought myself a pair of Adler Elevator Shoes (whose ads promised to make the wearer "Taller Than She Is"). That boost to both my stature and my ego seemed to help a lot!

In 1942, before I turned 22 years old, I had to have a third operation. I had finally had enough. I knew by now that I really wanted to sing, and this time, at my pleading, Papa finally agreed to shut the butcher shop.

I was free now to strive seriously for a vocal career. I came to New York and stayed at Salvatore's home in the Bronx on Murdoch Avenue. By now, Salvatore was quite successful, playing at Radio City Music Hall and in various radio orchestras, including Paul Whiteman's orchestra. He would tell me stories about how Mr. Whiteman himself would only show up at the end for the final rehearsal and performance, after his assistant did all the preparation work for him. Salvatore told me about the time Licia Albanese came as a guest artist to sing "Un bel di" with the orchestra. Mr. Whiteman apparently didn't understand the intricacies of Puccini's writing and the orchestra had trouble with a crucial cue played by two trumpets. Miss Albanese finally had to say, *"Maestro—in quattro, non in due!"* ("in four, not in two"). That miraculously solved the problem.

My other brothers, Nadir and Alfonse, were less adventurous. Both got married and stayed in New Haven, teaching and playing in local orchestras, including the New Haven Symphony. Alberto, now also married, moved to New London, Connecticut, and became head druggist of a large local pharmacy, but still always continued to play the piano whenever he was able.

For the following few months in 1942, I commuted almost daily to Manhattan from Salvatore's home in the Bronx, inquiring about upcoming auditions. I remember taking a few gratis lessons from a kind, elderly professor at Carnegie Hall Studios on the technique of singing popular music with a microphone.

Being overly ambitious, I auditioned for the Metropolitan Opera Auditions of the Air at an NBC studio. I sang "De' miei bollenti spiriti" from Act II of *La Traviata*. I had a lot of nerve. I thought I did well, but I didn't hear back from them.

Yost Music Management was looking for a tenor for their barbershop quartet. I got the job, but had to wear my elevator shoes so I could be closer in height to the other three singers. We sang for a week in an off-color nightclub in the vicinity of West 55th Street. I still remember quite a bit of dancing on the bar and a lot of hanky-panky going on during the proceedings.

Through the same Yost Management, I was accepted in the St. Louis municipal summer open-air operetta season for 11 weeks' work. The repertoire included *Desert Song, Rosemarie,* and *Show Boat.*

Being a habitual live-wire, I always managed to be chosen by the directors to perform small assisting roles in addition to my chorus participation. My salary was a whopping $110 per week—a really good salary at the time—and I always managed to send home about $90.00, because our room and board was included. We really worked for our money, though, with a change of operetta each week, rehearsals all day, performances in the evening, and a final dress rehearsal for the coming show all night long after the Sunday night performance. During the last two weeks of the St. Louis season, since we had no rehearsals and with only evening performances, I was able to get a part-time job in a local butcher shop. It not only kept me in shape as a butcher, but it also gave me some extra cash.

At season's end, I returned to New York with enough money saved to rent a tiny one-room apartment (about 8 feet by 15 feet) around the corner from Radio City Music Hall. I immediately started to look for my next singing job, and I went from place to place auditioning, always singing my favorite pieces at the time, either the *La Traviata* aria for tenor or "Dein ist mein ganzes Herz" from Franz Lehár's *The Land of Smiles.*

The Paper Mill Playhouse in Milburn, New Jersey, was putting out a call for their 1943 opening season production of *The Vaga-*

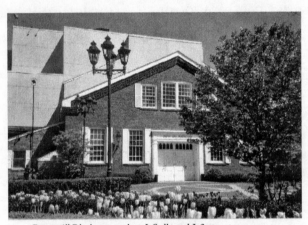

Papermill Playhouse—where I Sally and I first met.
Photo courtesy of Paper Mill Playhouse, Millburn, NJ.

bond King. I was lucky enough to get a job in the tenor ensemble. What a beautiful setting it was, located next to a stream, where I spent many of my lunch hours studying the score.

At the first musical rehearsal, I was seated on the aisle in the row behind the soprano section. Stretching my legs onto the chair in front, my foot accidently touched the derrière of—yes, you guessed right—Sally Bell, whose real name was Serafina Bellantone. The dark-eyed Latin beauty turned toward me with the meanest glare, which seemed to say, "How dare you?" I quickly apologized.

That same afternoon, the choreographer staged an apache dance routine for the wild Act I tavern scene in *The Vagabond King.*

As fate might have it, the director chose two Latin-looking types— yes—Sally and Tony. The routine consisted of pulling Sally away from a drunken lover, throwing her to the floor and, finally, kicking her. At every performance, immediately at the end of the Act, I quickly would inquire, "Did I hurt you, dear?" This gradually started a deep friendship, with the two of us always talking about our plans and the love we both had for opera.

Since Sally also lived in New York City, after the show, our routine was that we'd both board the train from Milburn to Hoboken, then take another train to the Hudson Street Tunnel station in the East Village. The time by now would be past midnight. I would accompany Sally home to 25 Charles Street, where she was living— five flights up—with her mother. I "conveniently" gave up my uptown lodgings and rented a room a few blocks away on Perry Street.

On our first official date, we stopped for a hamburger at a nearby White Castle. It was there I first proposed marriage and boasted that some day, instead of hamburgers, we would dine on steak and champagne. Her response then, as it was to be for about the next year, was always, "Tony, you're too serious; let's just be friends."

My first gift to Sally was a wristwatch, which she reluctantly accepted only after her

Sally at the Papermill Playhouse.

mother, Mama Bell, said, "It's only a gift of a friend; accept it." I was very fortunate in having Mama Bell on my side. Knowing I was low on cash, she'd always invite me to stay for lunches and dinners. Mama Bell and Sally for some time worked together in a dress factory on Bond Street, one block away from what would later become our 319 Bowery theatre. They were the sole supporters of the household, which also included Ma Bell's father, "Grandpop," who was 85 years old.

Blossom Time was the next production at the Paper Mill Playhouse; then it shut down for the winter months. I kept busy singing in church choirs and did some radio choral work, but I also spent most of my free hours auditioning and studying opera roles along with Sally. Our favorite duet was from *Lucia di Lammermoor*. She soon became an ardent opera lover.

By the spring of 1944, my finances were getting dangerously low. I began seriously thinking of going back to being a butcher again, but fate intervened. I was contracted for a 12-week summer operetta season in Dallas, Texas. Sally was now doing secretarial work in the law office of Mr. Bodin, in midtown Manhattan. Mr. Bodin was an opera lover who eventually joined the Amato Opera board as legal advisor.

On my last day in New York before leaving for Dallas, Sally took the afternoon off and we celebrated with lunch at Longchamps, which was a pretty classy restaurant. I wore my only suit for the occasion. We didn't have steak and champagne as promised on our first date at White Castle, but we did enjoy lobster thermidor and a glass of wine. Sally then accompanied me to Penn Station to board my train. It was a memorable afternoon. I was so happy to feel, for the first time, that Sally wished I didn't have to leave.

The Dallas season was a long, hot summer. I wrote a lot of letters to Sally—and she always wrote back to me. At the theatre, I made contacts with famous directors and started making new friends. One famous conductor from the Metropolitan, Giuseppe Bamboschek, took a liking to me and would

Me (far left) with my colleagues in Dallas.

choose me out of the ensemble for assisting roles. It was on Maestro Bamboschek's recommendation that, on my return to New York, I began to get singing engagements with established opera companies. I got wonderful experience that summer in Dallas. Singing in so many different shows under the direction of renowned musical and stage directors from the Metropolitan and Broadway musicals gave me the opportunity to learn through observation. Besides studying, you could say it took a lot of close attention (and a little stealing) to build my own style. All of this gave me the knowledge and confidence to carry through on my belief that opera on stage should also *always* be good theatre.

At the end of the Dallas season, I rushed back to New York, running to Charles Street, up five flights of steps, and into Sally's embrace. I was very happy for this reception. Distance had made the heart grown fonder.

Back in the fall of 1943, through a colleague, I had met Mr. Mario Pagano, a most humble and kind voice teacher. His wife Alice directed an opera class in a Brooklyn music school. I remember that it was at one of these classes that I observed a know-it-all director staging Leporello's "Catalogue Aria" from *Don Giovanni*. I thought he was wasting a whole lot of time on nonsense. It was then that I first thought, "I could do this!" When I came back from Dallas, the Paganos were preparing a presentation of Flotow's *Marta* and they invited me to sing the leading role of Lionel and direct the staging. This episode, with Mr. Pagano's encouragement, started me thinking of adding opera directing to my repertoire.

I also sang many Saturday evening performances at the Brooklyn Academy of Music with the Salmaggi Opera Company. Alfredo Salmaggi, the last of the old-fashioned opera impresarios, produced opera for many years at the Academy and filled the void of opera at popular prices.

It was always a miracle to me how the veteran conductor, Maestro Simeone, always held the Salmaggi productions together. Many future opera stars began their careers there, including Herva Nelli (Toscanini's favorite soprano), who sang *Aida* and *Forza* for

That's me (center, with arm outstretched), singing the role of Lionel in Marta, *1944.*

Salmaggi. Richard Tucker, the leading Metropolitan Opera tenor, also got his start in these productions.

Maestro Salmaggi was a tall, brawny, dark-complexioned gentleman who always wore a huge cowboy hat, a string tie, and carried a cane. The rumor in the trade was that, during his private coaching sessions, the sopranos usually got a good workout being chased around the grand piano.

Believing in my ability, Salmaggi, who had a very busy schedule, would say things to me like: "Amato, put together *The Barber of Seville* and do it next Saturday night up in the mountains, open air." He would give me a budget to work with, and I would take a 20-piece orchestra, and sure enough, we'd put on an opera a week later at one or another of the mountain resorts.

My next engagement that season was eight weeks of operettas in Detroit in the huge Armory auditorium. One episode I recall was when a highly-spirited member of the company, whose grandfather was an official in the Canadian government, invited some of his colleagues—me included—to a late-night, spicy party at his home in Toronto. Rum was the main drink. Being a non-drinking guy, I got terribly ill, putting me out of commission for about four days. I missed the dress rehearsal for the opening of the next show, which happened to be *The Vagabond King*.

Knowing there was a section with no action in the tavern scene, the choreographer gave me the OK to ad-lib the same apache routine I did at the Paper Mill. I had gained something of a reputation for my creativity on stage. The routine went over great and we repeated it to great acclaim for the remaining two-week run.

It was during this season that Maestro Bamboschek, again a guest conductor in Detroit, was putting together a troupe for an eight-week tour in the autumn of 1944 of *La Traviata* for the Wagner

Opera Company, featuring Metropolitan artists. I was flattered and surprised when Maestro Bamboschek assigned me the task of selecting 12 singers for the ensemble worthy of being hired. I must admit I chose my closest friends for the tour, but they were all capable singers with good voices. I was contracted to sing in alternate performances the roles of Gastone and the Marquis (a baritone role) and topping it all off, Maestro Bamboschek asked me to conduct the backstage choral number in Act III. Here again, not realizing it, I began my conducting career. It was a great feeling.

Back in New York, ready to start our *Traviata* rehearsals, my biggest hurdle was to convince Sally to become a member of the company. At first, she absolutely refused, saying she was being hired because of my personal interest, not on her talent. After much persuasion, especially from Mama Bell, Sally finally consented.

The next problem soon arose when the Bell family, along with Sally, decided that, for propriety's sake, we should become engaged before the tour began. Of course, this is what I was hoping for all along.

I should say a word or two about the extended Bell family. Sally's father was a shirt maker who had moved the family to Cohoes, up in the Albany area, when the company he worked for left New York City. After a year, Mama Bell, believing in Sally's theatrical career, had come back with her daughter to New York, so Sally could continue studying.

Once it was clear that I wanted to marry his daughter, Sally's father came back to the city to question me before giving his permission. I remember Papa Bell asking me, "Antonio, what will you do if you can't support my daughter with your singing?" I immediately answered, "I'll go back to being a butcher." And I meant it. That was the end of the family's objections.

In the fall of 1944, along with our colleagues, we began the strenuous, but fun time of the Wagner Opera tour of *La Traviata*. Many times, the local newspapers would feature a photo of us, with the comment that Sally and Tony were newly engaged. It made us sound as if we were starring in the opera. During this *Traviata* tour, we became close friends with a member of the ensemble, Joe Milly, whose father was the pastor of a Greek Episcopal Church in the East Village in New York. We had already set our wedding day for January 1st, 1945, and now we asked Father Milly to administer the wedding vows and his son to be our best man.

Finally, the time had come for Sally to meet my mother and

Sally and I during our dating days. I am wearing my one and only suit.

father. It happened on the closing night of the *La Traviata* tour in Bridgeport, Connecticut, not too far from New Haven. My father quickly took a liking to Sally; however mother was very cold to her, thinking of her as just a 'showgirl.' The real reason was that she was afraid she would lose what little earnings I sent home weekly. So, it wasn't a successful meeting. But this didn't change our plans for the wedding.

I was determined to give Sally an engagement ring. I picked out a beautiful marquise diamond that she loved. The ring cost close to $500, which I didn't have, so I asked my folks for my family share from the sale of the butcher shop—the same amount of money that my brothers received for their wedding gifts. Times were hard, though, and it wasn't easy for my family to agree. This problem was resolved when it turned out that my eldest brother, Salvatore, owed that exact amount to Papa. So, to keep peace in the family, all agreed that Salvatore would give me the $500 as my wedding gift.

We did have a lot of fun during the *Traviata* tour. The leading tenor, Armand Tokatyan of the Metropolitan, was quite a prankster, and he loved to play jokes on the cast during the performances. During a vital stage entrance, his favorite trick would be to make his entrance from a different side of the stage at every performance, confusing everyone on stage and making all of us run around to find our places.

To my surprise, once we returned to New York and before the wedding, I got a number of engagements for November and December. One was for a new musical on Broadway, *Sadie Thompson*. Once again, I had to be fitted with special high-heeled shoes. The show closed after only three weeks.

I also did two performances of Peppe (Harlequin) in *Pagliacci*, one in Washington, DC and the other in Baltimore, starring Giovanni

Martinelli as Canio. I found it puzzling when, during the performances, Martinelli, a former clarinetist, was clearly having trouble finding his notes and needed certain pitches on some recitative entrances, which were given to him on a pitch pipe from the stage wing by his personal valet and secretary. Of course, these performances were at the end of his career. For many opera fans, his tenor quality was not to their taste—but what a great line of legato bel canto singing he possessed, not to mention the chiaroscuro he applied to the lyrics! Do listen to his recordings of the two tenor arias from *Andrea Chenier.*

Next came a contract in Boston for one performance of Goro in *Madama Butterfly,* one of Peppe, and one of Schreiber in Wagner's *Tannhauser* (my first German singing role). The conductor was a Maestro Knopf, rumored in the opera circle to have been an illegitimate son of Richard Wagner. When I entered the conductor's studio to audition for him, I was stunned by his resemblance to Wagner himself. After singing through the role of Schreiber, I apologized for my German diction. I remember him saying, "No, no Amato. It's gut!" That was rather amazing, since I had only had three weeks to prepare for the audition. I got myself a self-taught German language book, a German-to-English dictionary, and took one $5.00 language pronunciation session—and then off to the audition.

***

Our wedding ceremony on January 1, 1945 was very simple, but memorable. That afternoon, while waiting for the family to assemble, Grandpop Bell kept repeating, in Calabrese dialect, "*E quando s'mang'?*" ("And when are we going to eat?") After the ceremony, we had dinner at a restaurant at 23rd Street and 8th Avenue. My brother Salvatore and his wife Tina joined us—the only representatives of my family. Mama was still angry with us. I must mention here that, two years later, we made my mother and Mama Bell very happy by remarrying at the Roman Catholic Church of Our Lady of Pompeii on Bleeker Street.

For our honeymoon, that evening we boarded the milk train (the only one available) to Hanover, New Hampshire. We chose Hanover because it was our favorite stop on the *Traviata* tour. The six-hour train ride was cold and uncomfortable, but we cuddled to keep warm. We arrived at our hotel in Hanover at about 2 AM, only to be told that they only had one room available—with twin beds. In the morning, knowing that we were newlyweds, they graciously changed our accommodations to a large double-bed suite. On Sally's persistence, we ice skated daily. The peace of this old New England town impressed us so much that, on our 20th anniversary, we revisited Hanover for our second honeymoon.

Back in New York, our honeymoon over, Mama Bell, worried about our financial situation, invited us to move in with her into her fifth-floor apartment on Charles Street. Once again she proved to be "La Salvatrice della Patria" ("The Savior of the Nation").

Our wedding photo, January 1, 1945.

Part II: Building an Opera Company

W HEN I look back to the first months of marriage, I'm always amazed at the many different ventures I undertook to begin building a good life for myself and Sally. If something came up that brought in a paycheck, I'd take it, even if it meant learning a new skill on the job.

Soon I began to get engagements in more prestigious opera circles. Through Maestro Bamboschek's recommendation, I was contracted to sing and stage manage a four-week tour of *Don Pasquale* with the Salvatore Baccaloni Opera Company, featuring the famous Metropolitan Opera buffo bass himself in the title role. At this point, I didn't have a lot of experience doing stage managing, but, as usual, I had watched others do it and figured I could do what was required.

It was the custom for the local management to plan a company party after the evening's opera. Mr. Baccaloni always insisted I sing his favorite Neapolitan song, "Marechiare," at these parties. Proud of his Italian artistry, Baccaloni was a perfectionist. He'd often say, "Amato, there are only two people at the Metropolitan who sing perfect Italian diction—Albanese and me!"

The business manager of the company, Mr. Pisano, made a big impression on me. Whenever he had his shoes polished for the going rate of 25 cents, he always gave a $2.00 tip. He would say to me, "Tony, remember, you must always go first class."

That spring of 1945, luck was with me. The Metropolitan Opera was still on their spring tour, making Alessio De Paolis, the

Metropolitan veteran comprimario tenor, unavailable. In his place, I was contracted to sing El Remendado in the RCA recording of *Carmen*, featuring Gladys Swarthout, Ramón Vinay, Robert Merrill, Licia Albanese, and conducted by Erich Leinsdorf, for many years a leading conductor at the Metropolitan Opera. During the rehearsal, Leinsdorf had trouble coordinating the orchestra in the *Carmen* quintet. Sometimes it happens that the singers have more knowledge about a particular style than the conductor. It took Miss Swarthout, with her veteran experience, who very diplomatically indicated to him how to work out the difficult rhythmic problem in the quintet.

Next came a short New York state tour of *Cavalleria Rusticana* and *I Pagliacci* (*Cav & Pag*) in the role of Peppe and *La Traviata* (Gastone). The young Nicolas Rescigno was the musical director, of whom I will say more later on. I was lucky enough to have worked with him at the beginning of both of our careers.

Finally, both Sally and I were hired as soloists for an eight-week, open air, summer season of operettas in Toledo, Ohio. I also doubled as stage manager. Singing and working together with Sally was like a second honeymoon. At times, I behaved like a typical jealous husband, especially when the conductor, Karl Kritz, flirted with my Sally. It started me thinking that perhaps that was why he made me sing a special solo number at every evening performance!

Back in New York with no engagements in sight, my colleagues—all novices in opera—encouraged me to start an opera class. I rented a dance studio for two months for a total cost of $100.00 and that was the start of the Amato Opera Workshop.

At about this time, the American Theatre Wing was opening a school for veterans under the G.I. Bill of Rights for study in ballet, drama, and opera. Norman Kelley, a tenor friend on the Metropolitan roster and a great "politician," invited the director of the school

Arriving in Toledo: Sally and I are in the front row, far right; behind Sally to her left is our friend John Costellano, and the Metropolitan Opera conductor, Karl Kritz, is center right, in a hat and smoking a cigarette.

to one of my opera classes. Pleased with what he saw, I was offered the position of director of the opera division of the school. At the same time, I was offered a six-week tour singing Goro in *Madama Butterfly* at $200 a week. During World War II, *Madama Butterfly* was not performed in the United States, presumably because of the plot, which involves an American navy lieutenant romancing an "enemy" Japanese girl. But now it was being scheduled again, giving me a chance to perform my favorite role of Goro, the Japanese "match-maker."

While hesitating before coming to a decision about what direction to take with my career, I sang Goro in a performance with the Connecticut Opera Company in Hartford, featuring the Met and movie star Nino Martini in the lead role of Lieutenant Pinkerton.

Mr. Martini received $2,000 for the evening's work, while my salary was $75.00! The next day, the reviews were quite negative for Pinkerton—and quite good for Goro.

After that performance, it was time for me to do some serious thinking. Always worried about having security for the future, I needed to make some decisions about what to do next. I weighed all the possibilities. Much as I loved to sing myself, I recognized that I wasn't all that happy with the complicated dealings required to advance through the ranks as a singer. Although I was finding jobs as a comprimario singer, I wasn't sure that this was the path I wanted to follow for the rest of my life. And trying to make it as a principal singer presented a whole new set of obstacles, dealing with people with huge egos, and a tremendous amount of politics. It was also clear to me that stage directing and conducting were becoming increasingly more important to me and that I found them both extremely gratifying and creatively satisfying.

After much thought, I made my decision to accept the teaching position of Opera Director with the American Theatre Wing Professional Training Program and not to take the six-week *Butterfly* tour. This was to be an important decision for me that would alter the course of my life. Weighing all my choices carefully, it seemed like the right thing to do to satisfy my own ambitions and provide financial security for Sally and me.

From the very first registration, about 40 G.I.s enrolled. But with only one female veteran, a soprano, we invited five talented students from my summer opera class to fill the female void. They were Sally, my dear wife, who has always been my leading prima donna, a great singing actress—the Callas of the Amato Opera. I also invited Dolores Mari-Galdi, my first Violetta, under scholarship coaching with Metropolitan conductors and leading soprano at the New York City Opera and San Francisco Opera. From the very start, Dolores assisted in all facets of our work and a lifelong friendship evolved. Ann Glisci Florio also joined us. She was a member of the Metropolitan ensemble for 30-odd years. Her spontaneous and emotional singing always made the audiences stand up and cheer. For the lower female voices, we had Anna Carnevale— a true contralto, a great Azucena—

Giving a fencing lesson.

who always assisted us in the costume department. If you want to hear a Neapolitan song sung correctly, Anna is the one who can do it. Finally, there was Pauline Kane, a real novice in opera with a

Teaching the minuet for Manon.

fantastic mezzo soprano voice, who became my favorite Amneris in *Aida*. She managed the costumes for 25 years.

With the steady and secure income from my teaching, Sally and I felt ready to leave Charles Street and move into our own apartment. In 1945, we purchased a co-op on West 45th Street, with plans that I could also teach privately there. Once we were in the new apartment, Papa began to make many trips to New York to visit us. He especially enjoyed auditing my opera classes. At times I would see him drying his eyes, overjoyed or touched watching me teach. In turn, we made regular visits to New Haven. Mama and Papa really got to know Sally and a great relationship of love and respect grew between them.

Unfortunately, our neighbors in the co-op were not happy with all the singing coming out of our apartment. After six months of complaints, we sold the co-op in the spring of '46, luckily with no financial loss.

Our next location was a large loft on 52nd Street, near Radio City Music Hall. The rear end of the studio became our living quarters. We turned the main front section into a mini-theatre, with stage, lighting, and accommodations for 30 guests whenever we gave studio showings.

As the classes got larger, I realized I needed more musical and language preparation. You could say I was teaching only with a "natural flare." I immediately began to re-study the operas I thought I already knew.

Remembering the admiration and respect I felt for Maestro Nicholas Rescigno, whose father played trumpet in the Met orchestra, I began to coach some of my opera scores with him at a very reasonable fee of $5.00 per hour (unbelievable nowadays). His insights and knowledge have been of the greatest help in my teachings.

His most precious story was from Act II of *Tosca*. Baron Scarpia is the much-feared chief of police in Rome at the time of Napoleon's 1800 invasion of Italy. Scarpia summons the beautiful diva, Floria Tosca, to his apartment at the Farnese Palace. He has arranged to have her lover, Mario Cavaradossi, tortured in an adjoining chamber on suspicion of shielding an escaped political prisoner. Scarpia's dual purpose is that Mario's screams will coerce Tosca into revealing the hiding place of the fugitive and, also, to force her to submit to Scarpia's desire for her. In his perverse brain, Scarpia wants Tosca all the more if she is helpless and full of loathing for him. He declares that he will spare Mario's life (a promise he has no intention of keeping) on the condition that she surrender herself to him.

At this point, Tosca has reached the emotional breaking point. Scarpia approaches her and softly, insinuatingly, utters one word: *"Ebbene?"* ("Well, then?") and waits for her response. Without having any lines to sing, Tosca reluctantly, shamefully nods, silently agreeing to yield herself to Scarpia in exchange for Mario's life. It is a brief pantomime, poignantly conveying Tosca's total helplessness in a situation so dire that words cannot even be formed.

Musically, as Maestro Rescigno explained to me, when Scarpia asks *"Ebbene?"* (page 254, Ricordi edition), the orchestra quotes the church theme of Act I in the two bars that follow. Tosca looks to heaven, as if she is saying to God, "Forgive me for what I am about to do." At the end of the first bar of the *andante mosso* that follows, she nods her head with shame, consenting to Scarpia's desires. The last note at the end of that bar is 'A' (in solfeggio, 'la') and the first note of the next bar is 'C' (or 'do'). Those two notes correspond to the Italian words *"la do,"* or "I give it."

Maestro Rescigno eventually became the music director of

the Chicago Opera and the Dallas Grand Opera. In his later years, he conducted at the Metropolitan Opera. He retired and went to live in Italy, where he passed away in 2009.

Passing on my experiences to my students, my ritual was: When learning an opera score, 1) Stop listening to the recording; 2) Get a good Italian-to-English dictionary; 3) Circle in your score the English equivalent with the foreign word. By seeing both the Italian and the English together, it helps to improve your vocabulary. For example, *Un* (one) *Bel* (fine) *Di* (day) *Vedremo* (we will see); 4) Work with a language teacher; 5) Solfeggio the lyrics with the correct rhythm; 6) Start singing the lyrics—a tempo; 7) Now—and only now— you can go back and listen to the recordings. Perhaps now you can start adding your personal spontaneity and individuality to your singing and make the music come alive for the audience to enjoy.

I was surprised to find that students didn't study solfeggio the way I had learned it, voicing aloud the subdivision of the value of the notes. The way I had been taught, the rhythmic values were clearly voiced, so that, for example, a dotted quarter note C would be practiced as "do-oh-oh."

This meant that the rhythmic values would become set in my mind at the same time as I was learning the basic score through solfeggio. Subconsciously, this method teaches the student to give the full even value to every note in the score.

For the next two years, the 52nd Street studio served us well, until one winter night in 1947, at about 2 AM, when we were awakened by a loud crash on the fire escape adjacent to our bedroom window, followed by heavy footsteps. Scared to death, we got dressed and caught a cab back to Mama Bell's apartment. The following day, when questioned by the police, we learned that, in the apartment above ours, the husband had come home unexpectedly. We always did suspect some hanky-panky was going on above us. We never slept there again.

Our next studio was a fourth-floor walk-up at 43rd Street and 6th Avenue. Again we turned the loft into a mini-theatre, with a full schedule of opera classes and rehearsals for our many engagements doing performances at local schools. The studio soon became packed with costumes, props, and lights. Luck again came our way. Our downstairs neighbor, Mr. Cohen, a businessman dealing in restaurant equipment, came up to investigate the "strange" noises coming from our studio. He soon became an opera enthusiast and a regular auditor of the opera classes. Observing our lack of space, he offered us the top two floors of his storage building at 319 Bowery free of charge. Not only did we now have storage space, but we also had a place to build sets. At that time, we never imagined that this building would one day become our own theatre.

It was time now to incorporate as a non-profit organization and, in 1948, the Amato Opera Theatre, Inc. was founded. Looking back on it today, it is very gratifying for me to know that we would go on to present literally thousands of performances to the public of more than 50 of the great operas in the repertoire. We also served as an experimental theatre in producing operas of Giuseppe Verdi, as well as other composers never or rarely performed in the United States.

Another important feature of our company was that we always kept our general prices affordable for the general public. Even more importantly, Amato Opera Theatre provided a testing ground for young singers seeking training and experience in the standard repertoire that would eventually provide their livelihoods. Many of our singers would go on to sing in the finest opera houses in the world, including the Metropolitan Opera and New York City Opera. Among those singers were Mignon Dunn, George Shirley, Neil Shicoff, Chester Ludgin, Robert Dunlap, Jerry Lo Monaco, Albert Da Costa, Jon Frederic West, and Tatiana Troyanos.

The tenor Jon Frederic West, who specialized in German repertoire, started his opera career with us. Then he went to Euroope and eventually sang a *Tristan und Isolde* at the Met when he was on their roster. He did not forget us though, and in 1993 said in an interview for U.S. Air Magazine:

> The Amato still stands as one of the greatest training grounds for singers. Tony has a traditional concept of opera that is real and alive.

Pauline Kane (one of our mezzo-sopranos who also worked

in the costume department, as mentioned before) reminded me recently about a fitting problem they had when Tatiana Troyanos (who started out in our *Carmen* chorus) sang Cherubino with us in *The Marriage of Figaro*. With so many performances and singers to accommodate, costuming could be catch-as-catch-can in our company, and, in this particular instance, Sally and Pauline couldn't come up with a shirt to fit Tatiana's long arms. They even tried shirts that Chester Ludgin wore, but that didn't work either. Through the whole ordeal, Tatiana remained patient and uncomplaining. After working with us, she went to Europe, where her career began in earnest.

When Sally and I made our first visit to Venice, we went to hear Nicolai Gedda in a church concert. Imagine our surprise when we saw Gedda sharing the stage with Tatiana! Afterward, she greeted us so warmly. It was a great loss to the operatic world when she died of pancreatic cancer at much too young an age.

Now that we had an "official" company, we needed a place to perform. I guess you could say that my mother, Maria Amato, and Mama Kate Bell were always looking out for us, for when, to please both of them, we "remarried" at the Roman Catholic church of Our Lady of Pompeii in the East Village, we developed a friendship with Father Louis, the priest who officiated at our Catholic ceremony. We thought that the church auditorium would be a good place to produce operas. An opera lover himself, Father Louis agreed and offered the space to us for a reduced fee.

On September 14, 1948, *The Barber of Seville* opened our season to favorable reviews. *The New York Times* took note of our new company in capital letters:

> AMATO OPENS TO LARGE AUDIENCE. Staged with
> verve and finish which made matters clear even to one not
> versed in the opera language.

The next production, *Cav & Pag* (*Cavalleria Rusticana* and *I Pagliacci*) was scheduled to open two weeks later. While preparing for the production, we made the acquaintance of Shelly Bartolini, an artist painting scenery for an Italian drama group using the same church auditorium. For days, Shelley watched our amateurish attempts to paint our sets. Finally, realizing we were in trouble, he shouted out in his high tenor voice, "Tony, go to your studio and teach your opera class. Come back at 5. I'll have the set finished." And he did! The *Cav* set was fantastic—all done with scrap pieces and an old dropcloth. This was the beginning of a lovely friendship. Shelly was our set designer for the next 20 years, until his union work and rules prevented him from continuing.

We followed *The Barber of Seville* and *Cav & Pag* with *Don Pasquale*—featuring Sally and Tony in the leading roles. Again, *The New York Times* had kind words for the production: "Costumes, make-up and stage direction were superior." The season closed with *La Traviata*.

Encouraged by the favorable reviews and the public response, the second season opened with a giant of an opera—Verdi's *Aida*. For this production, Shelly brought in his whole family to assist with the sets and costumes: his wife Denise, his dad Cesare, his sister Fiona, and her husband Dan—all very talented artists with their own particular styles. You can imagine the arguments that erupted, but

Photo: Marge Martin

Shelley Bartolini's set for Cavalleria Rusticana.

Shelly always had the final say. The *Aida* costumes were made from silver foil, buckram, and muslin, with painted Egyptian symbols. The choreographer of the ballet was—Tony Amato. In the triumphal scene, I liked the idea of telling the story of the opera through dance and pantomime, and reenacted the *Aida* plot, complete with a battle scene between the Egyptians and Ethopians and the love intrigue. The audience loved it. We got very good notices, including the *Daily News* critic Douglas Watt's comments:

Sally and I in our 1949 Don Pasquale.

> Village *Aida* A GOOD SHOW. This is traditional opera, done with taste and insight.

Louis Biancolli of the *New York World-Telegram* had particularly nice words for the show:

> Small scale 'Aida' goes over big. The opera was run off in lovely and artistic style . . . it is easy to see Signor Amato loved opera in general and 'Aida' in particular. Every phrase was stamped with the words 'con amore,' and enthusiasm radiated from him like a blessing.

We finished off the season with *Rigoletto* and *Carmen.* We felt like we were definitely on our way—until bad news came from Father Louis, who was always supportive and generous to the Amato Opera. Our Lady of Pompeii church was in need of funds, so opera got bounced out in favor of more lucrative bingo games. We had no choice but to go back to the studio. Once again, we needed to find a place to perform.

The next big venture in the spring of 1950 was a Mozart festival at Washington Irving High School. Within a period of a month, we did two performances each of *The Marriage of Figaro*, *The Magic Flute*, *Don Giovanni*, and *La Finta Giardiniera* (in its American premiere). For each opera, we had to build sets, design and make the costumes, and train singers—especially for the premiere. But the work never fazed us, nor did we stop to think what a huge undertaking this was. The festival received much recognition in the New York music circle. The *Herald Tribune* noted our premiere:

> The Amato Opera Theatre completed the first round of its Mozart series last night with 'La Finta Giardiniera'— Yesterday's well unified performance had a commendable general vocal standard.

The New York Times noted that

> The brave little Amato Opera Theater, which has been mounting works grand as well as small with slender resources since 1948, has set itself another significant challenge: its first summer season. . . . This is relatively fresh material of

Carmen *at Our Lady of Pompeii, with Madeline Vose as Carmen.*

a kind that benefits from the Amato's intimate yet exuberant style. . . .[*La Finta Gardiniera*] is entertaining and sometimes hilarious, but also appropriately touching.

In the summer of 1950, Sally and I decided it would be a good idea to have a place to live that wasn't just an alcove in the middle of all the teaching and production work, and we moved into a new apartment at 15 Sheridan Square. It was to be our home for the next nine years. Of course, Shelly Bartolini insisted on decorating it. On the bedroom wall, he painted a dream sequence of semi-veiled nudes reclining in a moonlit flower garden. On the living room walls was a panorama of the Act II Christmas crowd at Café Momus from *La Boheme*, and the room featured a convenient portable mini-bar. My guests enjoyed the bar décor the best!

Happily and comfortably settled in our new apartment, the search for our own theatre began. At 159 Bleecker Street, an old movie house renovated into a proscenium theatre by an Off-Broadway company became available. At first, the landlord, a *paesan* who had apparently had bad financial dealings with the previous theatre group, was adamant about not selling to another such group. But when I proved that, as a teacher on the American Theatre Wing staff, my income alone would sustain the mortgage payments, he finally agreed. And so, with our life savings of $10,000 and with a mortgage of $40,000, we had a theatre with 299 seats, a manually revolving stage, and lighting fixtures ready to operate. It was a lot of money, but I didn't give it a second thought, because it was the chance I was looking for to run our own theatre.

Soon after we moved in, we rented out the theatre to another company for one-night-stand shows. For the $100 fee they were paying us, I had to perform landlord duties when the gels on one of the lights needed refocusing. To do this, I had to climb up a 25-foot

Here's the proof that, even 50 years later, I would still be found up on tall ladders.

ladder to work on the light. I was plenty scared. There was nobody else I could get to go up and take care of it, so there was no choice but to do it myself; however, after that experience, I never was afraid again, and I ended up spending lots of hours in my life on the top of very long ladders. On November 25, 1950, after a long illness, Papa passed away at the age of 67. I regret that he didn't get a chance to see the Bleeker Street theatre in operation. And I never did locate his well-worn Italian books on Shakespeare and Dante that he so enjoyed reading. Mama and Papa had been living in New Haven with Alfonse and his wife Nancy. For a while after Papa's

My mother.

death, Mama maintained her own apartment and visited regularly with her five boys. Later, we convinced her to come and stay with us in New York. And what a joy and blessing it was to have her greet us with her Amato smile when we came home after the evening's show—and a home-cooked meal ready on the dining room table. (Mama cooked the best chicken cacciatore!)

It was to be a good time for Mama as well. All the time we were growing up, she was the linchpin of our family. She alone performed all the chores required to bring up an all-male family in the U.S. and took care of my father's sometimes excessive demands, as he, in old European fashion, expected his wife to cater to him without question. And still, she never once complained about the constant noise emanating from the various rooms in which we practiced our music. She was always ready with the proper excuse, too, when we did something that would displease our father. In Mama's later years with us, she took full advantage of being a 'free' woman, and she really started enjoying life.

During the first four months of 1951, it was full speed ahead preparing the theatre and the production for the opening Bleeker Street season. All members of the family joined in to help, each

Sally and I preparing for production at the Bleeker Street theatre.

with their specific responsibilities and duties. The two mothers concentrated on keeping the theatre in shape and ran the concession, featuring espresso and cannolis. Sally's older sister Margaret managed the box office and sales, was the hostess, and served as house photographer. Her other sister Annette (Annie) ushered and sang in the chorus. Soon the Amato Opera was referred to as the "Mom and Pop opera." Margaret's son Richard, who from his very first role as Butterfly's child showed his theatrical talent, became the company's leading bass-baritone, staged many of our operas (including our 1991 premiere of Martin Kalmanoff's *The Empty Bottle*), and appeared in Broadway and off-Broadway productions. It was always my hope that Richard would someday inherit and continue the Amato Opera. I regret that it didn't turn out that way.

With our opening of *Barber of Seville* already set for June, 1951, the stage union notified us that we had to have a union contract, the reason being that the previous tenant operated under the union's jurisdiction, which automatically made the theatre a union house. This meant we would have to hire union stagehands, electrical technicians, ushers, house managers, box office staff, etc. In my two meetings with the union committee, I tried to explain that the Amato Opera Theatre had a non-profit status, serving as

Photo: Marge Martin

Bleeker Street theatre: Sally as Norina, Don Pasquale

an opera school for young singers. My pleading was all in vain.

With their decision still pending, we had a difficult choice to make if we were going to open on time. I came up with an idea and went ahead and began the Amato Opera's first season, in its unauthorized union venue, on June 24, 1951. My creative solution to the problem made big news when we announced: FREE OPERA. As long as we didn't charge admission, we felt free of the union's restrictions. All seats were reserved, with a voluntary contribution after the first act. The result was a full house at all of our shows. The average contribution was between 40 and 50 cents—not enough to meet the expenses. We quickly changed the system by making the patron's reserve ticket an envelope with their name and seat number on it. After my first act speech, the envelopes were collected with the contribution enclosed. The average contribution then rose to $1.00 per person. When we opened the envelopes, occasionally there would be nothing but buttons and nails, but it also meant that we would sometimes find a five dollar bill nestled inside.

Don Pasquale *at the Bleeker Street theatre.*

Photo: Marge Martin

Looking back now, the decision to present free opera turned out to be a good gimmick. It attracted new audiences, and the result was full houses with standing room at all performances. At first, the union was angry with us and even did some picketing in front of the theatre, but after a week or so, they seemed to forget all about us. Our singers, who were getting invaluable training, had to be careful, though, and some of the union singers adopted 'stage names' for our productions, just to be on the safe side.

Soon, the reputation of the company grew as the word spread about the "GI performers." College music graduates began to come to us for opera training in the standard repertoire they needed to learn for their future careers. So, the company gained many new singers, who all wanted to be included in our productions.

To meet the mounting expenses, the company had to present more opera performances, more rehearsals, and more opera classes. The repertoire had to be enlarged and new sets and costumes had to be built. We ended up producing quite a number of operas in the course of the next year, including *Don Pasquale, La Traviata, La Forza del Destino, Aida, Il Trovatore, the Barber of*

Photo: Marge Martin

Sally (Susanna) and Dolores Mari-Galdi (Countess) in The Marriage of Figaro.

Seville, Cav & Pag, Carmen, Faust, The Marriage of Figaro, The Magic Flute, Don Giovanni, Rigoletto, and *La Boheme.* When I think back on it, I'm still amazed that we pulled it all off!

A *Marriage of Figaro* story from that period involves my dear friend Ann Boney. From the very beginning at Bleeker Street, raging storms never stopped Ann from driving 100 miles from New Jersey into Manhattan in time to perform whatever duties she committed to in the theatre. She wore many hats: a leading mezzo-soprano, box office manager, and a great organizer for our many fundraising affairs and galas. I shall never forget when, in her first performance as Cherubino in *Figaro*, the stage had been recently waxed. With much enthusiasm, she began her run to jump on a stool at far left stage for her big Act I solo. She slipped, fell on her derrière, but

"What! Disgraceful! A chambermaid at Prince Orlovsky's party!"
Ann Boney (l., arms outstretched) as the prince in Fledermaus.

Photo: Marge Martin

never missed a beat of her aria, "Non so piu." To avoid future falls, Carol Jensen Doubleday, one of Ann's close friends, who for many

Grabbing a nooze whenever (and wherever) we could.

years was a stage manager and prop director, immediately at intermission wiped down the floor to a dull finish. For years, Carol built and created many props that are still in use. Another thing about Ann Boney that I must mention is that, knowing my weakness for sweets (I do have a serious sweet tooth), through the years, Ann always supplied me with special pound cake she made with a particular flour she gets from down South, not to mention that they were the biggest pound cakes you could ever imagine. In the autumn, she would bring me luscious baked pears glazed with honey. No wonder I have a soft spot for her!

All of our hard work didn't go unnoticed in the press. *The New York Times* wrote about that first season's *Marriage of Figaro*: "The details of Anthony Amato's staging was a joy throughout." A 1952 *New York Journal American* feature story said:

> Music critics and big opera talent scouts who have seen Amato conduct have pronounced 'Tony' a real genius both as a musician and organizer.

With such a heavy schedule, the work crew of two—myself and stage manager (and baritone) Hank Kaufman—usually worked into the night. I must mention here that Hank Kaufman was the sweetest, kindest, and most soft-spoken 6'8" Texan you could ever meet. I shall never forget one late work night. When we finally left the theatre, the time was about 3 A.M. While Hank was locking the theatre gate, two strangers started pushing me and frisking my pockets. Hank quickly pulled me away from their grasp and, together, we started running down the dark street. The chase went on for about two blocks, with lots of punching and pushing. Being the smaller guy, I was getting the worst of it. Hank, in his calm legato (I love to use musical metaphors), lifted each of the two attackers one at a time and threw them against the parked cars nearby, putting them out of commission.

The following evening, while having dinner at Rocco's, our favorite neighborhood restaurant, the proprietress inquired about my cuts and bruises and I told her all about the incident. Late that same evening, Mrs. Rocco came to the theatre and in a mysterious, low voice (what we musicians call 'sotto voce') said, "Tony, you'll never be bothered again by any strangers." That's how we learned that we now had the protection of the local Mafia!

On a much-needed pasta break.

Part III:
Vacation Time & the Bleeker Street Theatre

WITH performances running continuously from September through June in the Bleeker Street theatre, we didn't have much time left for ourselves. Even when the theatre was dark in July and August, we were busy preparing for the coming season. Somehow, though, we managed to go away a few weekends to Fire Island for the fishing and swimming that Sally loved so much.

In the summer of '55, a lead soprano, Florence, invited us for a boat ride on her husband's 28-foot Cris-craft. We loved it. Without giving it another thought, within the next month we bought an old 30-foot Richardson and docked it at the Manhattan 79th Street

Sally, my brother Albert, and me on the 'High C.'

boatyard on the Hudson River. We named our boat 'The High C'—as we continued to call all our boats over the following years. Many nights, after the evening opera, we'd rush to 79th Street with a few of our colleagues and take a midnight ride up to the George Washington

Clowning around on the boat.

Bridge and back. Another exciting boat trip was up the Hudson, going through many locks, and, finally, to Albany. In addition, each Labor Day week, there was always a boat trip to New London to visit my brother Albert with Mama Bell and the rest of the family. All of this provided us with joy and a welcome change of pace.

We soon befriended an elderly sea captain, John, who taught me much about the boat— steering, docking, buoys, wind direction, etc. Under his direction, we went up to the Bronx to City Island for a Sunday picnic on the boat. As usual, I learned by watching the experienced Captain John navigate and thought I had the route down pat. The following Sunday, feeling very confident, we set off to

I don't know who was attached to the mysterious leg, but Sally doesn't seem very concerned.

City Island on our own, with our very dear friends Dolores Mari and her husband, Tony Galdi.

As a point of interest, to get to City Island, one goes up the Hudson River into the Harlem River, then to Hell Gate in the East River, and, finally, into the Long Island Sound. All was going smoothly until the boat went over a rock in the East River, making a crunching sound that we all knew was bad news and damaging the keel so it was impossible to steer in a straight line. We zigged and zagged to City Island, so that the 60-minute trip took us four hours.

We left the boat to be repaired at the boatyard and spent the remaining part of that Sunday exploring the Island. Sally and I fell under its spell. It reminded me of Minori, my birthplace, with all the boatyards and limited traffic. Both of us shared in comparing it to a sleepy New England town. It was amazing to us that, only 30 minutes away from the city, we could leave the hustle and bustle of Manhattan behind us in City Island. What a change for us from our busy work days and nights.

Once we came back to the city, we couldn't get memories of City Island out of our heads. We came up with the idea of buying a house there, where all the family could enjoy the boat and sea air together. Pooling our resources, Sally and I, Mama Amato, Mama Bell, and Margaret and Richard Martin purchased the waterfront dwelling at 606 King Avenue, City Island, the Bronx.

Four families in one house! We were all so busy working all day at the theatre that it never occurred to us to think this was a strange or dangerous arrangement. Surprisingly, we all got along and all enjoyed the home to its fullest, especially the fishing from the dock and the great outdoor Sunday family dinners prepared by the two Mamas, usually seafood (bass and lobsters) caught from our

The house at King Avenue, City Island.

Our backyard dock.

All the Bell girls (l. to r.):
Margie, Ma Bell, Annie (Annette), and Sally.

My brothers and I at Mama Amato's 80th birthday. (l. to r.): Alphonse (trumpeter), Salvatore
(oboe and flute), Mama, Nadir (flute), Tony-the-Factotum; and Albert (pianist and coach).

waterfront dock. On the rare times we all got to be together at the house, it was great fun to swim and eat together. And it never even occurred to us that having two mothers-in-law in the same house was something of a novelty!

Me and Mama Amato.

I even grew to enjoy the drive in and out of the city. Ever since that very first day, I always greet the spot on the East River where the boat ran into trouble with, "Hello, Tony's Rock!"

Fishing for dinner.

- 55 -

One of the unexpected advantages of our home on City Island was the new people we met. It takes a while for the insular City Islanders to accept newcomers, but we soon had new friends who welcomed us to the neighborhood.

The beginning of an improbable lifelong friendship with Frank Szymanski started in a typical way on City Island, where neighbors' chit-chat goes a long way in spreading the word about good people available for jobs and services. This particular story started on a sunny mid-August day, with the Amatos taking a rare lazy day at home listening to some lesser-known opera recordings. Outside in the garden, a young man recommended by a neighbor, Lois Dunton, a mezzo-soprano singing with our company, was cutting our lawn for the first time.

With the windows wide open, the sound of the electric lawnmower was coming through loud and clear, overpowering the recording. Minutes later, there was an abrupt stop of the motor. Curious to see if there was a problem with the lawnmower, I approached the garden window and, to my amazement, standing under the window was Frank, peacefully enjoying the opera being played inside. My first question was, "So, you like opera music?" His response was, "Oh yes, my favorite opera is Boito's *Mefistofele*." My reaction was, "Whoa, this guy must be a musicologist to know and enjoy this rarely-performed opera."

As we continued the conversation, I learned that his mother was working at the New York City Opera, which was presenting *Mefistofele* at that time. So, whenever he picked up his mother from the evening show, he would go backstage to enjoy the opera. Living only 10 minutes away in Throgs Neck, Bronx, Frank soon became one of the family. Going clamming at a nearby island and trying to beat Sally in Scrabble were two must-do activities whenever he joined us for Sunday dinner. Today, as I write, it has been 39 years since we met. I'm so proud to have him as my closest friend. P.S. Frank's second most favorite opera scene (can you believe it?) is the humming chorus from *Madama Butterfly*.

Frank's own story about how he came to meet us for the first time is a very funny one. As he tells it, while doing yard work for Lois, she suggested that he call us,

Frank Szymanski

since we had been looking for a good person to help out. Long hours at the theatre didn't leave much time to tend to the grounds at City Island, and Lois had strongly recommended Frank to us to help keep our property in shape. So, first opportunity he had, he called our house and got Sally on the phone. "Hello, Mrs. Amato," he reports saying, "I understand you need some tilling done." There was a disturbing silence at the other end of the line. "No, no," Sally answered. "I don't know where you got this idea." "But your neighbor told me to call you about some tilling." "No, no," insisted Sally most vehemently. "I don't want anybody killed." Luckily, all three of us got past this initial—and disturbing—first encounter. I think this story just serves to prove the importance of good diction!

* * *

In 1959, the company was in its ninth year of free operas. Now that I am writing this memoir, I often stop to reflect on how amazing it was that we ever made it work. I learned all my stagecraft by just doing it—observing others to find out how to stretch the muslin on a set, etc. As with my musical career, I learned by watching others, trying it myself, making mistake after mistake, and finally getting it right.

Some of these errors were embarrassing, but they certainly taught me a lesson—like the time I decided to make life easier by switching the order of the two operas for back-to-back *Cav & Pag* performances. We had finished a late-night *Pagliacci* performance and were all really tired, so I thought I'd leave the set as it was for the next day's matinee and simply start with *Pagliacci* for a change, rather than taking the time to put back up the *Cavalleria* set before we left for home.

The next day, I went around to all the singers and made sure the stage crew knew what was going on. My preparations complete (or so I thought), I went into the pit, where the two pianists were already in place to begin. Up went my baton and I gave my dramatic downbeat for the rousing *Pagliacci* opening, only to hear my pianists begin to play the slow, soft prelude to *Cavalleria Rusticana*. The only people I had forgotten to warn were the crucial two pianists! There was nothing to do but stop, let them know about the change, and start all over again. I

The alley at the Bleeker Street theatre,
with paintings by Shelley Bartolini.

had forgotten my lifelong mantra: ALWAYS ANTICIPATE! I can assure you I never made that mistake again!

All through this time at Bleeker Street, the other thing that I often wonder about was how we ever managed to fit in so many outside performances. The company made 25 years of visits to New London, where my brother Alberto (now going by his anglicized name 'Albert') lived and eventually retired. It was only through Albert's efforts that these operas were so successful, as he managed all the advance publicity, ticket sales, local chorus preparation, and played in the orchestra during the performances. Topping it all off were the home-cooked meals his wife Millie prepared for all of us starving artists!

It was during these years that we began our Operas-in-Brief series, designed to introduce opera to children. We would take standard operas and cut them down to 90-minute presentations, complete with a script to inform our young audiences about what was happening on stage. The narrative was always interwoven with the action. We took these performances to New York City schools and community centers, and did a Saturday evening summer series at Sterling Forest, to give children a pleasurable entry into, and an understanding of, the wonderful world of opera. Under the sponsorship of New York University's Division of General Education and Dr.

Sally and Sidney Stockton in La Boheme.

*Sally as the frail
Mimi in* La
Boheme.

*Sally as a frisky
Musetta in* La
Boheme.

Rehearsal at Bleeker Street in preparation for a performance of Tosca *in New London.*

Tosca, *Act III, in New London, Connecticut,*
with Catherine Bunn (Tosca) and Thomas Lo Monaco (Cavaradossi).

Arlene Randazzo and Jerome Robbins in Barber of Seville, *Opera-in-Brief version.*

Ormond Drake, Dean at New York University and director of Town Hall, we presented a Saturday Operas-in-Brief series for 10 years at Town Hall on 43rd Street in New York City.

Over the years, the Operas-in-Brief became a very popular part of our work, and it gave me great pleasure to provide this unique contribution to the field of education. The program didn't go unrecognized in the press. *The New York Herald Tribune* said about our Town Hall program:

> Informative as well as entertaining . . . Anthony Amato's interweaving of narration and music is skillful—effective, simple staging. . . .

A feature article in *The Villager* noted:

> The saint of Bleeker Street this month is Anthony Amato, who produced a shortened and adapted version of Puccini's 'La Boheme' for 300 Lower East Side school children.

I never believed in playing 'down' to children. Instead, we always aimed a little above them and this approach always worked.

After performances of *La Boheme*, when greeting the children, we would find them with tears in their eyes from the effect of the production.

Our Opera-in-Brief programs were primarily geared for children, but I soon discovered that the shows attracted many times more adults than children, proving that these shortened versions served a necessary function for novice adult operagoers as well as children and young adults. Part of it was the lower prices (even in the later years, we charged a flat $15 for the Opera-in-Brief programs), making them accessible to many who couldn't afford the high prices of the big opera companies. With the English narration that we included, the Operas-in-Brief also made the program an easy way to learn about an unfamiliar opera, something many adults found very useful.

Some of the other outside performances we did over the next 10 years included a *La Boheme* at West Point (the first opera ever produced there); *Carmen* at Lehigh University in Ohio; *Rigoletto* in Manchester for the Southern Vermont Art Festival; *Carmen* at Symphony Hall in Newark, New Jersey; *La Boheme* in New Haven, Connecticut; and a series of operas at Syracuse and Rochester, NY.

Carmen at Lehigh University.

Photo: Paul Rosenblum

Dolores Mari-Galdi and Sally with a general and an official at West Point.

We received quite a lot of great press during this time. *The New York Times* review of our *Lucia di Lammermoor* production in 1954 said:

> The chorus sang with gusto. Mr. Amato's conducting had vigor and authority, and 'Chi mi frena' stopped the show just as it does at the Metropolitan.

In the same year, the *New Haven Register* praised our *La Boheme*:

> Amato is a conductor of great power. His contagious fire and enthusiasm carries the entire cast and orchestra with him.

The *New London Evening Day* wrote this about our 1956 *La Traviata*:

> Much of the success is due to the vigor and good musical taste of the young conductor and impresario, Anthony Amato. It was a pleasure to watch him: agile and energetic, sensitive to every nuance, controlling orchestra, chorus and individual performers with great skill.

Dolores Mari-Galdi and Chester Ludgin, Tosca, *end of Act II.*

Bleeker Street La Traviata *set, Act II.*

Photo: Marge Martin

La Forza del Destino, *Robert Dunlop and Soto Andrea.*

Faust, *Act I. Mephisto (center) is William De Valentine, bass, who made a fine career in Europe.*

I have to admit that I took particular pleasure in some of the reviews during those years. One was *The New York Times* review of our *La Boheme*:

> There was something peculiarly authentic about the performance of Puccini's 'La Boheme' . . . this was due to the fact that the company, as the name suggests, presented the work as theatre.

The other was a 1959 feature story by John Ferris in the *New York World Telegram*:

> . . . an impresario who single-handedly has probably done more than any man in New York to interest the public in living opera. . . .

One Amato Opera tradition that began at Bleeker Street was our gala celebrations, which always involved a full opera performance and a sumptuous meal of several courses served in between acts, making for a long evening of eating, drinking, and music. One of our most popular galas was offered on New Year's Eve, and we would usually offer a crowd-pleaser like *Die Fledermaus* or *La Boheme*. The main attraction of the event was always our 'famous' meatballs and tomato sauce, balloons that dropped down from overhead, and champagne—the last of which was served at the stroke of midnight, ending the evening with a spontaneous opera selection. It was a great evening of fun and fund raising.

The preparations and catering for 150 patrons at the many gala presentations were always made successful by the participation and excellent organizational skills of the officers of the Guild and Guild present and past presidents, including Frank Brandt, Bob Palucci, Jean Hastings, and Corinta Kotula. Even though there was a lot of champagne that was consumed at the galas, the Guild team kept

Lucia di Lammermoor *wedding contract scene, with Isabel Talkin (Lucia) and Willaim Diard (Edgardo) (center, left). William was a leading tenor at City Opera and became a celebrated teacher in Connecticut, where he would visit with my brother Albert. Isabel's estate later gave us $10,000 for a new production of* Don Pasquale.

Checking out the lighting for Aida.

Marriage of Figaro *rebearsal at the Bleeker Street theatre.*

Il Trovatore, *Act II. (c., facing forward) Irene Kramarich was a contralto at City Opera and was on the verge of being signed to the Metropolitan Opera roster when she tragically died at a very early age.*

amazing order. Somehow, even though people were eating and drinking in their seats, order was always restored in time for the next act of the opera.

And although the galas went on long into the night, the team stayed even longer. As much advance preparation as they did under the direction of Ann Boney (who shopped endlessly for these occasions), first preparing food and then making sure that the patrons were served, Mimi Di Simone, and (in later years) Helen Van Tine, Vera Asaro, Lorraine Davidson, and Anastasia Ponomarev (who also served as an excellent stage manager) always stayed for hours afterward cleaning up and removing all signs of food and drink and empty glasses so the theatre would be ready for the next day's performance.

One thing they never had to clean up was Sally and Tony's meatballs, because they were always all gone by the finale. Nobody ever got the recipe, though, since I promised Sally never to reveal the secret ingredient—and I never did.

***

We were producing about 180 performances a year at the Bleeker Street theatre and had become very popular, but, by 1959, being young—I was 39—and ambitious, I was not too happy with the continuing status of "Free Opera!" Because we didn't charge for tickets, the company was not recognized by our peers and the musicians as a professional venture. This always bothered me, since the word 'professional' always meant for me presenting productions of high standard and quality—not just when one receives a financial return.

I was determined to change the direction of the Amato Opera Theatre. During the spring of '59, a successful Off-Broadway theatre, The Circle in the Square, had to relocate, since their building

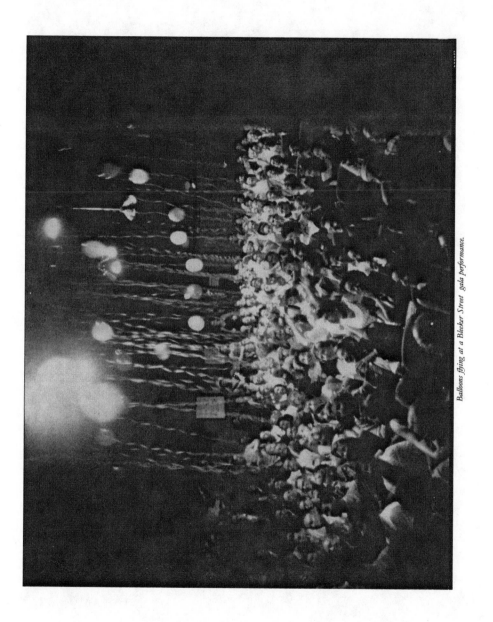

Balloons flying at a Bleeker Street gala performance.

Sally and Chester Ludgin, Manon, *Act I.*

Sally as Manon, Act III.

Sally in Lucia di Lammermoor.

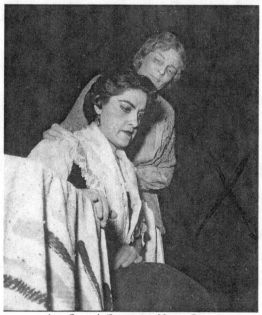

*Anna Carnevale (Santuzza) and Joanne Gregory
(Mama Lucia) in* Cavalleria Rusticana.

Bleeker Street theatre marquis.

was to be demolished. Just by chance, they inquired about the possibility of buying our theatre. Seeing the advantages of a financial opportunity that might support our future ventures, I agreed to sell. The 1959 season would be our last in the Bleeker Street theatre.

Closing day at the Bleeker Street theatre.

Part IV:

The Beginning and End of the
Professional Company, 1959 - 1963

SOON we were busy mounting professional shows with union contracts from a new studio at 126 West 23rd Street and Sixth Avenue, which was conveniently situated for opera classes and rehearsals.

Our first venture in 1959 was at a movie house in White Plains, NY, where we gave three Saturday evening operas, *Butterfly*, *Rigoletto*, and *La Traviata*. Our local 'impresario' was Lou Mattera, our legal counsel, who made all the business preparations for the theatre and never charged us a cent for his services. His continuing efforts on our behalf made these performances possible. The shows got very good reviews, but the box office was bad, and we ended up losing money.

Rehearsing at Town Hall.

The second venture was at the Kaufman Concert Hall, 92nd Street Y, in 1960. We gave a series of three Tuesday evening operas, *Rigoletto*, *Madama Butterfly*, and *La Boheme*. The result this time was good press and bad box office. Again, we lost money.

Next, our third venture was a revival of Verdi's *Luisa Miller* at Town Hall on May 21, 1960, starring the City Opera tenor Jerry LoMonaco and our own Dolores Mari-Galdi. We had very good reviews, good attendance, and almost managed to break even. The *New York Herald Tribune*'s Jay Harrison said about us:

> As presented by the Amato Opera Theatre on Saturday night at Town Hall, 'Luisa Miller' was revealed once again as a masterpiece . . . there are untold thanks due to Anthony Amato for presenting a Verdian stunner so long unavailable to Verdi-ites.

We next tried Verdi's first opera, *Un Giorno di Regno* in its American premiere, on June 18, 1960. We played to very good reviews, fair attendance, and—we lost money. Frances D. Perkins, of the *New York Herald Tribune*, said:

Town Hall rehearsal, 1960. My brother Nadir is playing flute and Alphonse is on the trumpet. They both came down especially to participate.

Keeping with the comic spirit of the show, I am joking with the orchestra during a rehearsal at Town Hall for Un Giorno di Regno.

The performance under Anthony Amato's stimulating conductorship, was spirited and well co-ordinated. . . .

In 1961, we did a revival of *Aroldo*, which is presented occasionally by the Met in a revival version known as *Stiffelio*. Once again, we had very good reviews, fair attendance—and lost money. The press was very complimentary about the production. The *New York World Telegram & Sun*'s Louis Biancolli said:

> Credit Anthony Amato and his stalwart little Opera The-atre with a courageous act of faith in Town Hall last night. What Mr. Amato did was to prove two things—that he had a good thing in his little Opera Theatre and that 'Aroldo' was very much worth hearing. These people love and live opera.

Elliot Stein, writing for the London publication *Opera* wrote:

> I attended seven performances at the Metropolitan this sea-son, and in spite of some fine individual singing, none of them seemed held together by anything more sturdy than the prompter's book and none could compare with this AROLDO. . . . It was stirringly sung, staged with great

beauty and imagination, and vigorously conducted by Anthony Amato.

It is worth mentioning that this performance marked the New York debut of George Shirley in the tenor lead. Shortly after this production, he received a Metropolitan Opera contract. Many years later and after great success, George answered an interviewer's question about highlights of his career by saying: "My most exciting experience was singing *Aroldo* with Amato Opera."

***

Soon there was news about a new organization, the National Music Theatre, which was being funded by its general manager, Horace Wolfson. He himself was an opera lover with ambitions of becoming an impresario. The company announced that they would produce a series of three operas, to be performed at Carnegie Hall, featuring international opera stars. Being familiar with my career and the work of our company, Mr. Wolfson engaged me to be the

Aroldo, *rehearsal, Town Hall, 1961, with Anne Ottaviano and George Shirley.*

opera conductor and stage director. The operas were to be Verdi's *Luisa Miller*, Franz Lehar's *Das Land des Lächelns* (*The Land of Smiles*), and Verdi's *La Battaglia di Legnano*. The orchestra was the renowned Symphony of the Air, Arturo Toscanini's orchestra. Now that Maestro Toscanini had retired, the orchestra was accepting outside engagements.

Needless to say, this was a very exciting venture for me, and a good boost to my ego after my years of "Free Opera." I thought this was the direction I wanted to take at this point in my career, and I looked forward to conducting at Carnegie Hall with such wonderful musicians and prominent singers.

On January 9, 1963, we opened with *Luisa Miller*, starring Dolores Mari-Galdi, Mignon Dunn, and Giuseppe Campora. Again we were reviewed in the London publication, *Opera* (Robert Sabin):

Verdi's 'Luisa Miller' at Carnegie Hall was a delight to hear

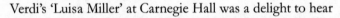

Rehearsal at Carnegie Hall.

Giuseppe Campora, Dolores Mari-Galdi, and I rehearsing in the 23rd Street studio for the Carnegie Hall Luisa Miller, 1963.

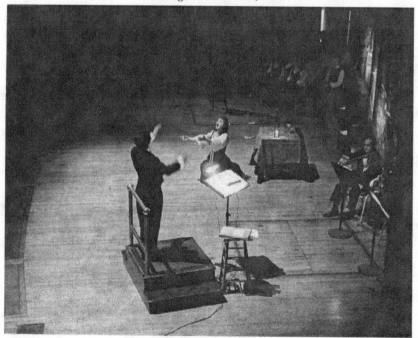

Rehearsing Luisa Miller at Carnegie Hall..

↙ Una is here somewhere

Luisa Miller at Carnegie Hall, with Dolores Mari-Galdi and Giuseppe Campora.
And, yes, though it might be hard to tell from this photograph, that is me conducting.

Rehearsing Lila Caputo and David Smith, both of City Opera, for Land of Smiles *at Carnegie Hall.*

and it was splendidly done. Careful rehearsal and thorough attention to detail had their reward. Mr. Amato conducted precisely but not pedantically; the Symphony of the Air musicians played con amore. .

However, a newspaper strike in New York hurt us badly, and the box office was not good.

On March 6, we played Lehar's *Das Land des Lächelns* to a sold-out house. It seemed that all of New York City's Germantown residents turned out to hear their favorite stars from Germany, Anneliese Rothenberger and Rudolf Schock. We were widely reviewed, including in *The New Yorker* and *The New York Times*. Miles Kastendieck of the *Christian Science Monitor* said:

> The indefatigable Mr. Amato conducted members of the Symphony of the Air with considerable zest and schmaltz. . . .

With the continuing newspaper strike in New York City, advance sales for *La Battaglia di Legnano* suffered so badly that, much to my regret, the decision was made by the financial backers to cancel the production.

The National Music Theatre's final venture was the farewell concert tour of the renowned tenor Tito Schipa. My brother Albert was engaged to be Maestro Schipa's accompanist—but not without quite a bit of effort.

When we first asked Albert to take the position, he immediately declined, since he had a good job managing the prescription department at a pharmacy in New London. He also expressed apprehension about appearing in such a major concert tour. However, I felt that he was uniquely qualified to take on this job. Tito Schipa spoke very little English, and would require an accompanist who could "interpret" for him. Schipa was also a diabetic, and my

"Let us get back to the old, it will be a step forward."
GIUSEPPE VERDI-(1813-1901)

OPERAS by Giuseppe Verdi		First Performance
OBERTO	Milan	Nov. 17, 1839
UN GIORNO DI REGNO*	Milan	Sept. 5, 1840
(Il Finto Stanislao)		
NABUCODONOSOR	Milan	Mar. 9, 1842
(Nabucco)		
I LOMBARDI	Milan	Feb. 11, 1843
(Presented as "Jerusalem"-Paris, Nov. 26, 1847)		
ERNANI	Venice	Mar. 9, 1844
I DUE FOSCARI	Rome	Nov. 3, 1844
GIOVANNA d'ARCO	Milan	Feb. 15, 1845
ALZIRA	Naples	Aug. 12, 1845
ATTILA	Venice	Mar. 17, 1846
MACBETH	Florence	Mar. 14, 1847
(Revised version-Paris, Apr. 21, 1865)		
I MASNADIERI	London	July 22, 1847
IL CORSARO	Trieste	Oct. 25, 1848
LA BATTAGLIA DI LEGNANO	Rome	Jan. 27, 1849
LUISA MILLER**	Naples	Dec. 8, 1849
RIGOLETTO	Venice	Mar. 11, 1851
IL TROVATORE	Rome	Jan. 19, 1853
LA TRAVIATA	Venice	Mar. 6, 1853
I VESPRI SICILIANI	Paris	June 13, 1855
SIMON BOCCANEGRA	Venice	Mar. 12, 1857
(Revised version-Milan, Mar. 24, 1881)		
AROLDO	Rimini	Aug. 16, 1857
(Originally "Stiffelio"-Trieste, Nov. 16, 1850)		
UN BALLO IN MASCHERA	Rome	Feb. 17, 1859
LA FORZA DEL DESTINO	St. Pet'b'g.	Nov. 10, 1862
(Revised version-Milan, Feb. 20, 1869)		
DON CARLO	Paris	Mar. 11, 1867
(Revised version-Milan, Jan. 10, 1884)		
AIDA	Cairo	Dec. 24, 1871
OTELLO	Milan	Feb. 5, 1887
FALSTAFF	Milan	Feb. 9, 1893

*American premiere by Amato Opera, June 18, 1960.
**Revived by Amato Opera Theatre, Inc., May 21, 1960.

*In 1960, we made this up as a bookmark for our patrons.
I still find myself going back to it as a reference.*

pharmacist brother Albert would make the perfect companion for him and could help maintain his medical regimen while they were on the road. As to Albert's musical qualifications, there was no doubt at all about his ability to handle the demands of this tour. All the same, it took Sally's repeated telephone calls to convince him that he was the man for the job.

Albert has reminded me about some of the events of the tour. Sometimes I caught up with them as they travelled all over the country—for example, in Philadelphia, Washington, DC, and Newark, New Jersey—but many of the things that happened can only be recounted by Albert. I pass on these stories, often in Albert's words, mostly to try to convey how difficult it can be dealing with "stars" and also to try to explain why the world of the lead singers proved less attractive to me than the life I chose for myself.

Getting ready for the first concert was already an indication of what was to come. Albert met with Schipa just two days before the concert was to take place. Schipa was willing to rehearse only two numbers before he stated that everything would be fine and that they would go over the rest of the program the next day. Then he requested that Albert lower the key of "Le Violette" by a half-tone, since he felt that the high tessitura was a little too strenuous. This was to be only the first of many similar requests—often at the very last moment—that he made during the weeks ahead.

As it turned out, Schipa found an excuse to cancel the second rehearsal, which meant that only two numbers had been prepared before we opened the tour on October 3, 1963 to a sold-out concert at Town Hall. There was an overflow audience of about 100 people who had to be accommodated on the stage. Schipa was enthusiastically received and he rewarded his audience with five encores. The after-concert reception took place at the Fifth Avenue

Walter must our wedding

apartment of Licia Albanese. It was quite an event, with many celebrities, including Franco Corelli, Giovanni Martinelli, and Walter Toscanini (Maestro Arturo Toscanini's son), among others.

Albert had been an admirer of Schipa's since he was a young piano student, and he particularly loved Schipa's recordings of the two arias from *Manon*, the *Marta* 'M'appari,' and arias from the *Barber of Seville* and *Don Pasquale*. He had started out on this adventure certain that such vocal artistry could only come from a person possessed of great sophistication and intellectual curiosity. Unfortunately, many of Albert's illusions were shattered in the course of the upcoming tour.

I can testify to one of the disappointing occurrences. During Schipa's appearance in Washington, DC, a whole group of us, along with our wives, dined at an open-air French restaurant. When

Tito Schipa at Town Hall, October 3, 1963, accompanied by my brother, Albert Amato.

the waiter recognized Schipa, he brought a bottle of fine French wine to our table, compliments of the management. After thanking the waiter, I picked up the bottle and began to fill the ladies' glasses. In an instant, Schipa grabbed my wrist and said, 'Me first!' Ever since then, this has become an Amato family joke. Each time wine is served, someone makes sure to yell out: "Me first!"

In each city in which Schipa appeared, there was plenty of attention from the press, with an obligatory interview. In Chicago, the music critic Donal Henahan asked to meet at a local hangout for musical artists, Italian Village restaurant, noted for its various nooks, like "La Taverna," where guests can be seated in privacy. As usual, Schipa opened the interview by announcing that he had two daughters—43 and 41—and "my wife 39."' Henahan looked at Albert quizzically, who had to explain that the tenor was now married to an exceptionally beautiful woman much younger than himself.

Henahan asked Schipa if he vocalized regularly to maintain his vocal health. The response was, "Me No Vocalize!" Through Albert, he explained that, when he got up on the day of a concert, he would first close one nostril and then the other and screech "EEEEEEE!" If the sound was clear, he would know that he was in good voice. He was then asked if he planned to return to Italy when his visa expired. Schipa responded that he would remain in this country and teach voice, which prompted Henahan to turn to Albert to ask, "What is he going to teach—how to EEEEEE?"

Before the interview, the waiters, who remembered Schipa well from his days at the Chicago Lyric Opera, told him there was a special party planned that evening in the restaurant to honor Carol Fox, General Manager of the opera. Then and there, Schipa decided to dine at Italian Village that evening. When he and Albert arrived, none of the celebrities seemed to be there. In fact, the staff was curiously silent and embarrassed. Schipa called over a waiter and asked where the guests were. The waiter sheepishly pointed to one of the restaurant's nooks that had been curtained off for privacy. It was clear that the party didn't want to be disturbed. Schipa got up, hobbled over (he had trouble walking), and pulled the curtain open. The response was one of utter surprise. After a "Tito, what are you doing here?" Schipa and Albert were invited to join their table, where some of the brightest stars of the day were assembled, including Renata Tebaldi, Tito Gobbi, and Boris Christoff, in addition to Carol Fox, various spouses, and the husband of Maria Caniglia the famous dramatic soprano, who was Fox' vocal consultant.

Despite the delicious food and wine and much conversation among the people assembled about appearing with Schipa during his later years, Albert sensed a lack of genuine friendship. Two evenings later, not one of them attended Schipa's concert. Maybe it was pay-back for Schipa not attending Boris Christoff's performance of Prince Igor (which featured Rudolf Nureyev in the Polivetsian dances of the opera). Albert had begged for a ticket, which was very hard to get, and Donal Henahan kindly provided tickets for both of them, but Schipa preferred to watch a "girlie" show at the hotel.

Other events of the tour included a stop for a lecture recital in Boulder, Colorado. Albert was worried about Schipa's ability to speak about his program as the booker had requested, but the tenor said not to worry. As they walked to the auditorium to begin the lecture recital, Albert reminded him once again about the format— only four songs, but with commentary. Schipa turned to Albert and said, "Me No Talk!'" When Albert asked him why, he said, "No In Contract." Albert quickly improvised the spoken part and, fortunately, the program went smoothly. Schipa even added two encores!

An interesting event took place during the tour's visit to San Francisco. Schipa and Albert were invited by the mayor of Oakland to a fundraising dinner for the Oakland Symphony. The guest of honor was the famous operetta composer Rudolf Friml. Schipa and Friml greeted each other like old friends, as they had been neighbors in Hollywood while filming movies in the '30s.

The host of the event was Ralph Edwards, well-known from

From the album cover of Tito Schipa's first concert for the National Music Theatre at Town Hall, with my brother Albert at the piano and some of the overflow audience seated on stage.

the TV program "This Is Your Life." The entertainment included Liberace's brother's orchestra, as well as a fine harp trio and dancers. It really didn't seem to make much difference who was performing, though, since nothing got through the clanking of utensils and the din of people speaking in loud voices. Then Ralph Edwards announced the presence of the renowned tenor Tito Schipa and asked him to favor the guests with a song. Albert's heart fell. He knew that Schipa did not perform without being paid. But it proved to be too embarrassing to refuse. Albert began to play the opening bars of "Marechiare." As soon as Schipa began to sing, the silence in

My brother Albert, Schipa's tour accompanist extraordinaire.

the room, as Albert put it, "became deafening." The ovation was tremendous and thrilling in response. Ralph Edwards could only comment to Albert in wonder, "Amato, this is extraordinary! We all tried hard to entertain, but no one would listen. The old man just opened his mouth and there was absolute silence!"

It was only when Schipa's brother, a publicity agent for MGM, flew in from Hollywood that Albert learned Schipa's real age. He had been "billing" himself as 64 years old. But when Albert asked the brother how old he was, he said, "I am 63—11 years younger than Tito."

His brother proved to be very useful in another way. Schipa had brought along a set of gray concert attire for the Sunday afternoon concert, which he had not worn for many years. However, when he put on the pants, it proved impossible to button them up in front. This provoked a few moments of anxiety, until his brother grabbed his pants and quickly tore open the back seam, assuring Tito that his tails would cover the breach!

The concert was a great success. Before they left, the brother confided in Albert that Schipa had always been involved with beautiful women and that he had squandered millions of dollars on his amorous escapades.

The tour finished with a repeat concert at Town Hall. This time, the reaction was very sad. The hall was empty. We apparently had run out of old-timers who were familiar with the great Tito Schipa. For those who were there, he sang arias from *L'Arlesiana* and *Werther*, along with a bouncy rendition of "Vivere" from his movie of the same name.

The tour over, true to his word, Schipa managed to remain in the United States and did some teaching. He died two years later and his body was flown to Italy for burial. The city of Bari honored him by naming the local conservatory of music after him.

My brother Albert returned to New London and went back to his career as head pharmacist—but not without many memories about his experience, many of which he has been kind enough to share in these pages.

As part of my compensation as manager of the tour, I was left with 1,000 Schipa recordings. Always one to make lemonade when left with lemons, my business sense told me not to despair. I paid the taxes on the recordings and sold them over the years at $10 apiece—and even made a small profit!

After this experience with the National Music Theatre, I had a great deal to think about. I had learned some important lessons about working with established stars, as opposed to my previous experiences directing young ambitious singers eager to learn and bring new ideas to life. I had to compare the excitement I was used to creating in the theatre with the many drawbacks of accommodating "stars," including limited rehearsal time, the fact that directions were often ignored, and that the celebrities were set in their ways. With their lack of cooperation on costuming and make up, it was impossible to achieve the kind of unified production I was accustomed to.

I came away from this experience convinced that opera on a limited budget can only be successful when one individual directs and controls the production, including the musical direction. Having done it this way for many years at this point, my decision then was to "Stay Small—but GRAND!" I drew comfort from a quote by Verdi himself: "Let us go back to the old. It will be a step forward!"

Part V
Amato Opera on the Bowery: 1963-2009

I T was time to go back to the drawing board. Sally and I knew that we wanted our own theatre again. Suddenly, it hit me: "Eureka!" Why not the free-rent storage building on the Bowery, where we had been making and storing our sets and costumes? Sally's first reaction was, "Tony, you're crazy! It's small, derelicts are always sleeping in front, and there is all the noise from the elevated train passing by. Besides, how do you know if the building is for sale?"

This is what 319 Bowery looked like when we bought it in 1963.

But luck was with us. Mrs. Cohen, now a widow, was interested when we made the proposition to her and, within one week, she decided to sell to us. We bought 319 Bowery for $22,500.00. That sounds like very little, but I knew it would cost a great deal to make over the space to fit our needs—a mighty task. In fact, it cost another $85,000.00 to turn the building into an opera house.

Being a frequent visitor and admirer of the Shakespeare theatre in Stratford, Connecticut, I copied (stole) some of their stage construction ideas for our miniature house. Then, we hired an architect to take on this challenge of turning the 110-year-old building of what once was the Holy Name Mission into an opera theatre. I

Photo: Erika Davidson

Preparing the second story studio floor for rehearsals and showcase performances.

That's me with the saw, building the stage, while Sally 'supervises' from the balcony.

already had many ideas about how we could transform the four-story building (22' x 125') into a workable theatre that might be tiny, but would have grand capabilities, and the architect was pleased to have a miniature cardboard set I made of the theatre, complete with a floor plan of the finished project.

The plan reserved the upper two floors for storage of 50 opera sets and costumes. The second floor held rehearsal space, a sewing room, chorus dressing rooms, and a private office. The cellar and part of the first floor were to become the 107-seat theatre. That meant cutting away much of the first floor. The cellar became the stage, room for 69 seats, a concession area, and the lounge. What remained of the first floor became a lobby, box office, and a balcony for 38 patrons. The part of the first floor that had been removed

Photo: Rineke Akkerhuis

The Bowery's backstage 'tunnel.'

created the theatre's height of 23' for artists to sing out unrestrained. The architect also carved out a 20' x 10' orchestra pit under the stage, *à la* Bayreuth,
which was used for special effects, and
then burrowed still further, leading the
way to a narrow, four-foot-wide, fun-
house tunnel to the backstage area.

But there was one further hurdle.
"What! An opera house with no trap
door!" How could there be such a
thing? In our shopping for a motorized lift, not only was it too
costly, but its size would leave no space in the pit for the orchestra
players. Once again we had a *Salvatore della Patria* come to the rescue.
Bill Thompson, one of our tenors and an aeronautical engineer at
Republic Aircraft (not to mention a boatsman and a great guy), designed a simple counterweight system operated manually. The cost
was cable, pulleys, wood, and metal hinges—for a total of $23.00.
Thank you, Bill Thompson!

Now we were all set for what would become some of our
signature stagings, including Don Giovanni's dramatic descent into
hell, a way for Dr. Miracle (one of the three villains in *The Tales of
Hoffmann*) to vanish suddenly, for a huge birthday cake to pop up in
the finale of *Don Pasquale*, and for the second act of *Tosca*, where
Floria Tosca is forced to watch through the trap door into the torture chamber below Baron Scarpia's office in the Farnese palace as
her lover is being questioned—a truly chilling effect with lurid red
lighting and smoke rising up from the orchestra pit. (How many
complaints I heard over the years from the orchestra players, trying
to read their music through the fog!) In the case of *Don Giovanni*, the

entire set crumbled before the eyes of the audience as the Don disappeared into hell, provoking astonishment and applause. No other alternative to that scene could possibly have been as theatrically effective as his plunge through that $23.00 trap door to Mozart's swirling, diabolical music.

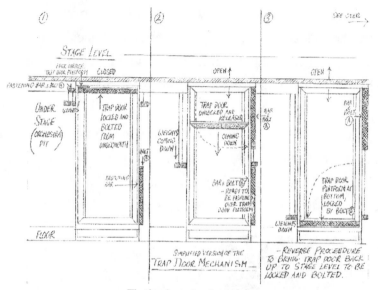

The plans for our ingenious trap door.

All was ready for our grand opening of *La Boheme* on September 11, 1964—except the necessary final approval from the New York City Department of Buildings. Without their permission, we couldn't open the doors. And they kept us waiting and waiting. It was a real nail-biter. We were down to the last day when the inspector finally came. He made his rounds, checked off each item on his list, and then turned to me as he was ready to leave and said, "Tony, you're trying to run the Metropolitan Opera in this small building!" But finally, with the necessary building permit proudly posted in the lobby, the curtain went up right on time at 7:30 PM. The way we did it was with two small chandeliers rising, on the style of the extravagantly elaborate Austrian crystal version at the Metropolitan. The reaction was the same that first evening as it continued to be for all the years that followed: the audience applauds. As Sally put it, "It's all tongue-in-cheek." My reaction was, "It's not the Met, but here we go!"

***

I think it is worth taking a moment to mention that there was a precedent for opera in downtown Manhattan. While many people are aware that Yiddish theatre, with its strong musical tradition, had a rich history just a few blocks away from us on Second Avenue, fewer people know that opera existed in the area as far back as the 1820s.

It all began in 1825, when the celebrated Spanish tenor and teacher, Manuel Garcia, brought his singing family to the old Park Theatre near Park Row and introduced opera to New York with the assistance of Mozart's legendary librettist, Lorenzo Da Ponte, who was now an entrepreneur and professor at Columbia University.

Our 'famous' chandeliers were also used in The Marriage of Figaro *sets, seen here from the left perch.*

Opening with *The Barber of Seville* and *Don Giovanni*, they were a considerable success. Garcia's daughter had a personal triumph. Later known as Maria Malibran, she went on to a brilliant career, adored in Manhattan, until her life was cut short at the shockingly early age of 28.

The time was now ripe for the amazing Lorenzo Da Ponte, who was now already 85 years old, to try his hand at becoming an opera impresario and, as usual, he invested his money and his heart into the enterprise. The Italian Opera House, which opened in 1833 on Leonard and Church Streets, was a handsome, neo-classic-style building. It was the very first theatre in the United States designed exclusively for opera and opera alone. The company imported Italy's best singers. Unfortunately (something I could well understand), at the close of the second season, the theatre suffered an overwhelming deficit and there was absolutely no forthcoming financial backing and had to close. Terribly disappointed, the once indomitable Da Ponte concluded that New York was far more concerned with profits than with culture.

Da Ponte lived for years on Spring Street, only a few blocks away from 319 Bowery. Since the spring of 2009, there has been a permanent commemorative plaque hanging on the corner of Church and Leonard Streets in Tribeca, inscribed: Lorenzo Da Ponte Way.

Also rather ill-fated several years later was Palmo's Opera House, built in 1844 on Chambers Street. The company's meager financial resources could not quite compete with the theatres that were bringing in big stars from Paris and Milan.

When the old Bowery Theatre came into being in 1826, the goal was to present some native American talent singing in English to a diversified audi-

The second of our two chandeliers, seen in The Marriage of Figaro *from the right perch.*

ence of both the wealthy and lower middle class. It was also the site of many a vehement abolitionist meeting over 30 years before the Civil War.

Continuing up the Bowery to East 8th Street, a magnificent edifice arose in the early 1840s. The Astor Place Opera was situated near what is, these days, a K-Mart. In its day, it attracted Europe's most illustrious vocal artists, until it was doomed by a politically- and ethnically-motivated riot. The theatre would remain in operation for a few more years, but it was understandable why opera singers would no longer even consider appearing there.

Niblo's Garden, on Broadway near Prince Street, fared much better, with a healthy run from 1830 to 1858. They served both opera in English and homemade ice cream in the garden. Sounds lovely! Even lovelier was Castle Garden in Battery Park, where Jenny Lind made her debut in 1850. It was a favorite hangout for America's opera-loving poet Walt Whitman, who enjoyed the cool breezes from New York Bay as much as the music inside.

Obviously, there was a long tradition of music-making flourishing all around lower Manhattan in the early 19th century—and there is actually a good reason for it. At that time, north of 14th Street, there was simply nothing but miles and miles of farmland, hills, thickets, and the occasional isolated country mansion. Fourteenth Street was considered uptown! When the academy of Music opened its doors there in 1854, it became the cultural Mecca of the city's "old moneyed" high society. Its snobbish elitism so frustrated the "new rich" like the Vanderbilts, the Morgans, and the Astors, that they resolved to have their own theatre constructed far uptown on West 40th Street—and that's when the Metropolitan Opera was born in 1883, marking the beginning of opera's Upper West Side migration.

So, without even knowing it at the time, Sally and I were

From an old postcard of the Amato Opera on the Bowery—early years.

carrying on a tradition that began nearly 140 years earlier. We might have felt like newcomers, but our vision of transforming an old factory-warehouse into a small, privately-owned opera company was actually not such a stretch, and was something that fit right into our new neighborhood on the Lower East Side.

***

What a luxury and a blessing it was once again to work and create in our own theatre. We could rehearse the cast with sets and lighting when it suited us and run rehearsals longer than originally scheduled. Best of all was the opportunity to keep on experimenting and improving whatever production we were working on.

One thing we had to fight in the early years at 319 Bowery was the neighborhood's reputation. In the beginning, the patrons feared coming down to the Bowery area. During the first 20 years, there were times when we were very discouraged. There were performances where there were more performers on the stage than patrons in the audience (I did like to use all the people who wanted to be part of our productions). Many times, when our spirits were low, we gave serious thought to turning the opera house into a dinner theatre. But, through our personal financial backing and by obtaining a small loan, we stuck it out and survived those lean years.

It took a huge amount of work just to get started in our new theatre. To make good of the minutely-proportioned stage, we had to rebuild all of our old opera sets to fit the smaller space. On a positive note, though, it gave us the opportunity to introduce new stagings and try out fresh ideas for our standard repertoire. And we had plenty of chances to show off our new theatre and new stagings that first year, as we undertook a ridiculously ambitious season of 10 productions, following *La Boheme* with *Die Fledermaus, Marriage of Figaro, La Traviata, Hansel & Gretel, Madama Butterfly, Aida, Barber of Seville, Luisa Miller,*

The Barber of Seville *set, with the doors closed for the Act II rainstorm.*

Sally (Rosini) and Max Frescolm (Figaro) on
the Barber of Seville *set, doors open.*

and *Magic Flute*. We never thought twice about doing so many shows, even though our schedule was quite demanding. Between each show, the previous opera would have to be struck, new sets put in place, and stage rehearsals for the next show completed in less than a week's time. In addition, we also offered a full calendar of Opera-in-Brief performances, including our regular repertoire, *The Mikado, Cinderella,* and highlighting a *Pied Piper* we commissioned from my staff conductor, Stelio Dubbiosi. And just so we wouldn't get lazy, we also offered an extensive Amato Opera Showcase selection of public events. It somehow seemed perfectly natural to us.

The first production to get a facelift was our bread-and-butter opera, *La Traviata*, soon to be followed by *Aida* and *Barber of Seville*. What we were doing was not lost on the press. Over the next few years, critics never failed to mention what was taking place on the Bowery. David Frost summed it up when he said:

> The Amato Opera House is a splendid example of enterprise in the unlikely purlieus of its tiny theatre on the Bowery. The performances have good standards; the casts are young and energetic and the seats are truly inexpensive. In fact, in many ways this is what opera really is about—and such surroundings clearly demonstrate that away from chi-chi environments, opera can stimulate curiosity, awe, entertain and communicate.

About our *Aida*, Edward Rothstein of the *The New York Times* wrote:

> . . . everything is proportioned for the space. The cloth backdrops can give a feeling of expanse, and though there is no doubting the obviousness of the artifice—there is no pretense here to verismo stagecraft—everything was worked on with such taste and care that Verdi seemed not only to survive, but also even now and then to thrive.

The small scale often worked to our advantage, as noted by R. Oestreich of *The New York Times*, in his review of *Barber of Seville*:

The Feisty Amato Opera—as intimate as the Met is grandioso—revels endearingly in the contrast.

Keeping in mind our past brushes with the union, and knowing that the singers' union would pick up on the fact that their union members were working with us, we billed the company at first as a showcase training program. Luckily, the union left us alone. Musicians were compensated with stipends, but, in the beginning, we couldn't afford to pay all the many people on stage.

In later years, we did offer a small stipend to the singers. Before each performance, it was a great pleasure for me to go backstage in my full-dress tuxedo to greet each singer and personally hand him or

Sally as Violetta in the last act of La Traviata in the Bowery theatre.

Our Madama Butterfly *set at the Bleeker Street theatre. Notice the two side pavilions, where I showed offstage action behind a scrim, including Butterfly's entrance and Suzuki's household preparations.*

Cutting down the Madama Butterfly *set for the Bowery theatre. The two side pavilions I liked so much were, unfortunately, the first to go.*

her their honorarium. Even though it was a small gesture, I felt it was important that each member of the troupe was treated with respect and thanked for their participation.

The Bowery theatre started a trend of attracting new faces who, beside their interest in opera, were seeking technical stage knowledge. Fortunately, many of them formed the nucleus of our stage staff and became valued members of the

Aida: (l. to r.) Thomas Lo Monaco (Radames), Sally (Aida), Anna Carnevale (Amneris).

Amato Opera family. And it quickly became just that—a family. Many people found a refuge in our theatre, where we spent so much time together that we felt part of whatever it was that brought people to our doorstep. Mostly people came because they loved opera and wanted to be part of our efforts, either by singing or helping with the technical side of the business. Some came because they were lonely or unhappy, and it made them feel good to find a place where they were welcomed and appreciated, and where they were not judged on problems they had or missteps they might have taken in the past. Our "Ma and Pa" company soon became an extended family, subject to all the love—and dysfunction—that such a family always brings along with it.

One of the earliest to follow us to the Bowery was Abe Londisky, who had turned up one day at the Bleeker Street theatre. He was a middle-aged gentleman, working nights at a printing plant in Brooklyn, but he spent most of his free time building and painting

Painting Pinafore sets with Bernie Goldberg. The second floor studio served double duty for the display of artwork.

miniature sets for our Opera-in-Brief repertoire. The *Hansel & Gretel* gingerbread house and Cinderella's carriage for the Massenet *Cendrillon*, which we performed in an English translation by the conductor Donald Meyers, were his work, and both served us well for many, many years. It was easy to make Abe happy— all I had to do was give him the opportunity to super on stage in our productions, which he enjoyed immensely. Abe met a sad end. One night, he was accidentally locked into the printing plant. Trying to get out by the fire escape, he fell to his death. What a loss to all of us who had come to love him.

Angela Varnadore, a ballet enthusiast and herself a dancer, choreographed many of our dance routines. Even though she had a full-time office job, starting in 1965 Angela would spend her evenings at 319 Bowery, controlling all the props and stage cues during all rehearsals and performances. Angela also sang soprano in the chorus and took on a number of solo roles with us. She eventually returned to her home out West, but she loved the stage so much, I'm sure her involvement with theatre continued.

Also joining us in 1965 was Bernie Goldberg. Bernie was living with his folks in Brooklyn. He had motor and mental problems that made a normal life difficult for him. All the same, he would wake up when it was still dark and take a long subway ride five mornings a week in order to be at work in a midtown Manhattan diner by 6 A.M. He performed his many duties for the early breakfast and luncheon crowd and by 3 PM every day, he would come to us to indulge his love of the theatre. His early studies on the violin gave him the basics to become the musical backbone of the chorus tenor section, not to mention performing various character roles. Even though Bernie's limitations hindered his personal life, for 33 years he was always there willing to lend a hand at whatever he could do to help at the theatre. I like to think that Sally and I gave him a purpose and a safe haven, and we often served as surrogate parents, giving him advice that would help him live a better life.

From her very first day at the theatre in 1970, Lucy Weed was an invaluable help. Lucy not only assisted in every facet of the theatre, but her extensive knowledge of the English language enabled her to produce English

Lucy Weed (l.) checking out cues backstage.

versions of Boito's *Nerone* and Ricci's *Crispino e la Comare*. For over 25 years, Lucy wore many hats in the Bowery theatre. She served as stage manager, chorister, stage director, my personal encyclopaedia, and company dramaturge. Anything I needed to know about historic facts or an English language question, she knew the answer.

Lucy was such an indispensable helper that I kept her in mind when constructing new sets. Since she was on the plump side, I had to make sure that the narrow passages backstage would accommodate her quick moves behind the scenes directing the action and making sure everyone was in the right place at the right time. Given the size of the theatre, that wasn't always easy. As anyone who has worked at Amato Opera knows, there were some treacherously small spaces in the perches and sometimes serving as entrances and exits between the sets. Outside the theatre, Lucy also served for many years as the director of a famous children's summer camp in Connecticut.

The Amato Opera was most fortunate the day in 1971 that Richard Cerullo walked into the theatre on the advice of an acquaintance. Even though he had a day job as a designer/painter for a big

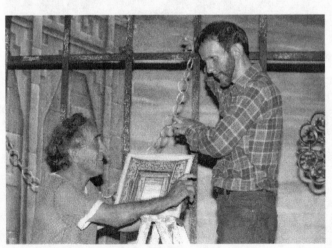

Working on sets with Richard Cerullo.

display company in Jersey City and was already painting sets for the old Jean Cocteau Theater located diagonally across the street from us, he quickly became

Act II Andrea Chenier *set by Richard Cerullo.*

Jerry Rizzo and Lois Dunton on the Act II set of Andrea Chenier.

our scenic designer. In no time, Richard was perched on top of a 12- foot ladder, ready to paint his first opera with us—*Andrea Chenier.* His enormous talent as a designer and painter, plus his vast knowledge of musical and historical information, made him the perfect person to be part of our efforts. He was able to make maximal use of our miniscule stage, and he created amazing, multilevel sets that are not to be forgotten.

Andrea Chenier isn't exactly standard repertoire,

Three of Richard Cerullo's sketches for The Tales of Hoffman*:
top—tavern scene; middle—Vienna; bottom—Venice.*

but ever since I was young and an ardent member of my school fencing team, I had always had loved stories about the French Revolution, like *A Tale of Two Cities* and *The Count of Monte Cristo*, and *Andrea Chenier* is the opera par excellence about that period of time. Musicologists have never been crazy about the opera, but it is a great theatre piece—and tenors love it for all the great patriotic arias they get to sing. Richard took to the piece immediately, and built beautiful sets for our production.

But that wasn't all that Richard did for us. Later, when I wanted to produce Verdi's *Otello* in English, he did the English translation for us of Boito's libretto, and he was able to blend the drama of the words with the music to convey the full emotion of both the story and the musical score.

As Richard pointed out when describing how difficult this translation task was, Italian is an expansive, poetic language, while English is heavy with consonants and blunt endings. The Italian for 'spring' is 'primavera,' a potential aria in itself with four syllables and four open-vowel sounds, while 'spring' is a one-syllable word with five consonants and only one very closed vowel. Richard didn't give up, though, and became obsessed with the project, scribbling away every day on the F train to and from his display job. Not being a musician, he hammered the music into his head at night after work. Being an opera fanatic really helped.

I loved the way Richard worked on translations: it was always his practice to provide me with three possible variations whenever a vocal problem presented itself, and he trusted me to make the final choice.

The critics praised Richard's work. When he did *La Traviata* for us, *Opera Monthly* wrote:

> . . . Cerullo's lavishly exquisite sets and costumes must have
> been constructed of miracles.

About his *Tales of Hoffman*, Anthony Coggi of WFUX-FM said:

> Richard Cerullo's designs were first rate . . . the best I've
> seen in many a production of this opera.

And that was only the beginning. Richard also directed a number of Operas-in-Brief for me, as well as presentations of Gilbert & Sullivan, including the rarely-performed *Ruddigore*. I was delighted and privileged to have Richard working with us from 1971 on.

One of the best and most loyal staff members I ever had started out by making not the greatest first impression on me. During the '81-'82 season, three young people showed up one day on our doorstep. I thought of them as three "Dead End" kids. Ricardo Figueroa struck me as a tough, African-American teenager, and he had in tow two street-wise fellow teenagers, Latina friend Vivien and hard-boiled Italian-American Tina. I figured they had come on a lark and wouldn't stay long. But after chit-chatting for a few minutes, I realized that these three were really interested and were sincere about wanting to involve themselves with opera. All three of them had good natural voices and wanted to be in the chorus, where they went on to take small roles.

Due to work and family obligations, Vivien and Tina eventually left the company after about five years, but not Ricardo (Ricky), who stayed on to be my right hand man for 28 years. From scrappy street kid, Ricky became a real gentleman. In addition to being the most reliable and artistic comprimario baritone in the company, Ricky never ceased to amaze me with his stage awareness and his ability to make quick adjustments on stage to compensate for errors commited by others in the cast.

Company members over the years grew to trust Ricky implicitly for cues and directions on stage. He helped everyone and grew to be beloved by the others, because they knew he was always there to provide support and a smile whenever a question or a problem arose on stage or backstage. In fact, when things got messy on stage during a performance, I would sometimes try to catch the eyes of my cast members, only to find that they were all looking at Ricky to solve the dilemma! But that was all right with me, because Ricky's eyes never left mine, and many a time we exchanged a knowing look

and I knew that Ricky would take care of a problem that I couldn't solve short of jumping up on stage myself.

Ricky did everything for me. His duties

At the back center of this photo is Ricardo Figueroa (Ricky), keeping watch—as always—over everybody on stage.

included: 1) stage manager; 2) prompter; 3) chorus member; 4) baritone soloist; 5) Sally's assistant with the lights; 6) working with the subtitles; 7) general house manager; 8) director of the backstage chorus. When he wasn't doing those tasks, he was cleaning up after a show or sweeping out the theatre.

In the beginning, there was some competition between Ricky and my other assistant, Bernie Goldberg, but they grew to be great pals, often going home to Brooklyn together on the subway late at night, sometimes accompanied by Richard Cerullo. I used to call Bernie and Ricky my "Mutt and Jeff"—and I certainly was lucky to have them both. In fact, without such a wonderful, loyal staff, I don't know how a normal "Day at the Opera" could have taken place.

Part VI:
A Day at the Opera

LIFE at an opera company is not for the faint of heart. Our typical day at 319 Bowery lasted 12-14 hours, 7 days a week. For Sally and me, it would start at 8:30 AM with a hearty breakfast at our favorite Columbus diner in the Bronx, followed by our trip from City Island into Manhattan. The 40-minute drive was always a convenient time to plan our itinerary for the day.

At 10:30 AM, I would drop off Sally in midtown at the New York Athletic Club for daily water exercises with some of our theatre patrons. Sally relished keeping fit, and this time spent at the gym would be her only free time of the day.

I would arrive at the theatre at around 11 A.M. and start in on my first job, which was to clear off and sweep the sidewalk in

Photo: Rineke Akkerhuis

In the costume room.

front of the theatre in order to make sure we didn't get violations or fines from the City Sanitation inspector. We had a rather raucous hard rock club next to us, the famous CBGB, and they often left the outside a mess. Once inside the theatre, it was time to set up the coffee and tea counter and make sure there were snacks for the singers rushing in from work for their 5:30 PM cast rehearsal.

The next regular daily job was

to check out the bathrooms and make sure they were spic and span. Then I would begin to work on setting up the stage—making sure I knew what flats, props, costumes, and other ac-

Believe it or not—opera necessities!

cessories I was going to need for the evening's rehearsal.

At 1:00 PM, Sally would return from the gym and we would take a break for our afternoon meal with food we had prepared that morning and brought in from home.

We would clear a space on the crowded office desk and sit down and try to enjoy our meal before the phones would start to ring with inquiries and ticket sales and the inevitable casting prob-

lems—somebody with the flu who couldn't sing that weekend; somebody else who had a family emergency and wouldn't be able to come in for that night's rehearsal. After a final cup of demitasse (one of our luxuries) for the pick-me-up we needed to get us through the day, we would clean up the remains of our meal, turn our "dining area" back into an office desk and go off our own separate ways to tackle our respective duties. For

Backstage

Photo: Rineke Akkerhuis

the rest of the day, we rarely saw each other until it was time to go home after the rehearsal, which usually meant about 11 P.M.

For Sally, her job meant wearing many hats: bookkeeper, treasurer, cashier, public relations director, preparation of the weekly opera programs, creating press releases, maintaining and updating our mailing list, and taking care of ticket reservations. That didn't include her role as costume manager, preparing the costumes for the cast rehearsing that evening, and thinking ahead to set up all the costumes that would be needed for the coming weekend's shows. But that wasn't the half of it. In such close quarters, with hundreds of singers to keep happy, Sally was also the resident psychologist, and she was a master at retaining peace and respect among all the members of the company. It boggles the mind how she handled all of it at one time.

As for me, I would go upstairs during this time to select the hundreds of costumes that Sally had helped me pick out—all in the

Sally at work.

Sally sorting out costumes and props.

correct historic period, of course, for the opera we were currently working on—that we needed for the upcoming production. Then I would have to get them carried downstairs, so Sally could keep track of the dozens of fittings, repairs, and alterations necessary. There had to be enough outfits for 25-30 choristers, as well as another pile for the principal singers. Because we had multiple casts, the costumes had to come in a range of sizes. Usually, we had a small, medium, and large version of each outfit.

On actual performance days, it was always Sally who was at the helm of the backstage costume operations. First there were endless hours of ironing and labeling of costumes for the various performers who would be singing. Sometimes there would be several costume changes per person. Nervous singers had to be helped in and out of complicated outfits.

Sally and I in the costume room.

The name of the game was Velcro and tons of safety pins. As Sally always said, "Without safety pins, there is no opera." If a zipper gets stuck when the tenor is about to run out onstage, you're in big trouble. Sally had a genius for knowing how to use a piece of Velcro and a couple of safety pins to save a singer from losing his pants. In a pinch, there was always a flowing cape to throw over a split seam at the last moment.

I don't think the audience ever realizes what it takes to make sure everybody looks well-pressed and presentable onstage, especially in such close quarters as our small theatre. If we pulled it off, it was because of Sally. Without Sally at my side, our company would never have succeeded. Not only did I call her "the Callas of the Amato Opera," but she was also the backbone of the theatre.

While Sally was taking care of her afternoon duties, I would be making sure everything was in place for both the new production that lay ahead and whatever was needed for that particular day. I would go up to the top floor, where all the props and gimmicks were stored. Two or three afternoons a week, I would have to fish out missing pieces from the 3rd-floor scenery room, where hundreds of flats were piled in stacks in order to make sure everything was in place when we needed it.

This is a good place to mention some more of Riccardo's

many responsibilities. Living in Brooklyn, Ricky, who would assist me all through the evening's rehearsal, would never get home before midnight. The next day, he would be back in the theatre in time for the dinner I would have waiting for him, and then come help me on the upper floors, making sure he carried down everything Sally needed in the costume room and lugging flats and cut-outs onstage for the upcoming rehearsal.

Once we had all the many separate pieces together that we needed on stage, many remaining hours would be spent rebuilding and touching up the sets and all the other phases of the production. While this was going on, Sally would be busy recruiting the volunteers she needed to help with costume preparation.

By 5 PM, it would almost be time for rehearsal. I would wash up quickly and perhaps have a cup of tea for a bit of energy. The singers would start to rush in from all over—some from office jobs in Manhattan, others from long train trips from wherever they lived or worked—in order to make the rehearsal on time. With brown bags of sandwiches from the deli across the way or Chinese take-out for a quick dinner, they were eager to start rehearsing. Many carried styrofoam cups of coffee, because one thing they weren't too crazy

about was the coffee I had waiting at the theatre.

But my troubles were only starting. It would be 5:30 and, "My God, who's missing?" "No pianist yet?" But, oh yes, it's Taya Shumeria sched-

Principals' dressing room.

Photo: Rineke Akkerhuis

Lucia di Lammermoor *rehearsal; Mary Ellen Schauber (Lucia).*

uled, and I knew in advance not to fret. She was a teacher in New Jersey, and if she made all the train transfers, she would only be five minutes late.

Say the opera in rehearsal tonight is Mozart's *Marriage of Figaro.* OK—I know Ricky would be ready with the lights and curtain ... but, what? There is no Figaro yet. OK. These Mozart opera rehearsals could go on for 5 hours and more. There was no time to waste, so I make a quick decision: "Let's jump to scene two and then we'll jump back to the opening scene when Figaro gets here." To keep things moving, one must anticipate and prepare for such problems that often occur in this type of operation. So, we're ready to go—when the doorbell rings and, yes, it's Figaro. I cue up the Overture. I know exactly how long it will take, so I tell the baritone rushing in, "Figaro, you've got four minutes to be on stage. Ready, everybody, for Act One!"

And so it goes on and on into the night. Maybe, for a good rehearsal, most of the lead singers will know exactly what they are supposed to do, and it will be the crucial secondary parts that will get us into trouble. Many a *Figaro* rehearsal, we would linger on, say, the gardener Antonio's entrance in Act II, or Barbarina's last act walk down the aisle in the dark, looking for the lost pin, that would stop us from moving forward. More times than I can count, we would spend half an hour coordinating the dancers and ensemble singers in the wedding scene. But that's all part of the night's work, and every single one of these pieces of the puzzle is necessary to make good theatre happen. The important thing was that the magic of Mozart would make the artists on stage forget their hunger and how strenuous their day at the office had been, and they would be enveloped in the magic world of grand opera. At the end, we would all be exhausted and excited at the same time.

For me, I never tired of the wonderful experience of working with young aspiring opera artists. How many times did I look to the conductor's pit to check the time and see that it was 11:15 PM, and, for example, we would have just finished rehearsing the devilishly difficult and magnificent fugue at the end of *Falstaff*. The singers would be dead on their feet, but if I suggested, "How about doing the fugue again?" all in unison would shout, "Yes! Yes! Yes!" By the

Checking a point in the score with my assistant conductor, Joseph Marchese. On stage (l. to r.), Darren Chase, Enrique Rexach, and Deborah Surdi.

Photo: Rineke Akkerhuis

Ensemble members getting ready for showtime.

time we would leave the theatre, everyone would be reenergized and still singing as they departed.

***

On show days, the routine was even more complicated. For our 7:30 PM curtain, it would begin for Sally at 5:30, when she would give a final check on all the reservations to be picked up at the box office. She then made a trip to the backstage dressing room to be sure all the costumes and accessories were hanging correctly for the principals: Are there clean stockings and shirts in place? Have the costumes been adjusted to fit the cast singing this evening? Are the make-up and wigs in place? And, of course, are there plenty of safety pins!

As for me, 5:30 was the time to set the music stands and chairs in the orchestra pit and check the orchestra parts for any key changes or cuts for the evening's cast. Sometimes Rodolfo in *Boheme* will take the Act I aria down a half-step, as will some sopranos for "Sempre libera," the Act I cabaletta in *Traviata*; then there are different musical choices singers will make in bel canto showpieces, like the *Lucia di Lammermoor* cadenza with the flute in the heroine's last act mad scene.

Next, I had to make sure the lights on the music stands and the piano were all working properly, adjust the sound system, set up the cameras for the videotape and the computer for the opera supertitles, and, finally, check out the light control boards for the proper settings to start the show. I always had to remind myself not to forget (and sometimes I did!) to lower the two chandeliers, so they would be ready for the pre-overture surprise, when we would raise them to the ceiling, *à la* the Metropolitan Opera.

I would then give a final check of the cleanliness of the house, making sure the aisles were cleared and the bathrooms clean and

Sally on the light board.

freshly stocked. That would complete my routine for the front of house. By then, it would be 6:30, when I would finally give the OK to the box office to open the theatre doors for the early patrons waiting to come it. Sally would be all set and ready to greet each arriving audience member with her beautiful, soft, warm smile.

At 6:45, the rest of the singers and staff would begin to arrive. By a half-hour before showtime, as a rule, the singers should all be in the theatre, ready for final make-up and costume fitting. Working with so many volunteers, this rarely happened, so this was the time when I would be frantically checking to see who was missing.

For my backstage staff, this was the busiest part of the evening. Everybody had to be in costume and the details (accessories, swords, jewelry, etc.) taken care of. Richard Cerullo's job would be to check the make-up on all the singers and do the character make-up himself, so everyone would be consistent as to the proper age, have the right moustaches, beards, and wrinkles, etc. He also had to make sure everybody was using the proper pancake base to blend with the lighting, not to mention arrange masks and other special effects, like the clown masks for the *commedia del arte* scene in *I Pagliacci*. Ricky would wait for me to give the 10-minute call to turn on the master stage lights for the opening scene of the opera. We would check to see that the nine members of our chamber ensemble had arrived. Usually, that meant flute, piccolo, oboe, English

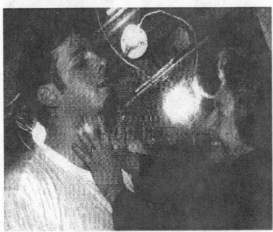

One place a safety pin won't work: Sally making sure a beard stays where it belongs.

horn, bassoon, first and second clarinets, trumpet, and French horn. Most importantly, I would have Ricky check that the pianist was in place, because, with our cut-down orchestrations, the main instrument playing the full score was the pianist.

On a not-infrequent night, it's ten minutes before the show and, say, for *Marriage of Figaro*, there is no Cherubino. She's on her way in from

Close quarters in the principals' dressing room.

Philadelphia, but her bus is stuck in the Holland Tunnel. I call for the Marcellina, who has sung Cherubino before, and quickly dress her in Cherubino's costume (mind you, she is about six inches taller than the scheduled singer). Then I grab a chorus member, who is already dressed and made-up as a flower girl. She is scheduled to sing Marcellina later in the run and I have the costume mistress quickly put her in the now-vacated Marcellina costume. Somebody else in the cast dashes over to turn the flower girl into a middle-aged matron with the quick application of make-up. Just as the curtain goes up, the original Cherubino dashes in, weeping and begging to be allowed to go on. The valiant chorus member is ripped out of the costume she is wearing and turns into a flower girl once again, rubbing off the "wrinkles" that have just been put around her eyes. Marcellina puts back on her original costume and goes running out on stage as Richard slaps some make-up on her before she makes her entrance. Luckily, it takes about 10 minutes before Cherubino needs to be onstage. A little frantic and worse for the wear, she makes it out on cue. Her tears have dried and she is ready to play a mischievous teen-aged boy.

This sort of thing didn't happen every night, but it certainly wasn't an unusual occurrence. This meant that I always had to anticipate who could cover (believe me, I had to keep this in mind when making up my cast lists) and I made sure there was always someone who could take over in an emergency—or myself. Many a time, Sally or I had to substitute in situations like this.

During the show itself, the staff managed the preparations and cues for entrances and exits and took care of quick costume changes that sometimes had to be done onstage during a blackout. Ricky would deal with backstage sound effects, like the first act *Otello* storm. He had a lot to do during that scene, including controlling the swinging boats in the storm. The ships were done with cut-outs attached to boards, which he had to move to and fro to mimic the effect of boats being tossed about in the storm. The staff had no time to rest.

Not all the crises we had to deal with took place onstage. There were also funny (or not so funny) things that would take place in the house itself. Once, during *La Traviata*, a derelict wandered in from the Bowery and made himself at home. Apparently he was an opera lover, and the events taking place on stage moved him greatly. Soon, we were all aware of the sobs coming from the audience. When he was approached by an usher, it was discovered that he had no ticket. But he promised to behave, so we let him stay to continue to enjoy the performance.

Another incident during a *Madama Butterfly* was both absurd and charmingly sweet, involving two geisha girls and a very senior citizen. The staging required Cio-Cio San and her geisha friends to enter in Act I from the back of the auditorium, then proceed down the center aisle and onto the stage to situate themselves on and around the upstage Japanese bridge, all while singing their beautiful entrance chorus. The timing wasn't quite on their side one evening because, as they were poetically gliding down the narrow aisle with their fans and parasols, an extremely geriatric lady with her cane to support her decided she needed the ladies' room immediately, causing a rather

Me (r.), pinch-hitting in the bass-baritone role of Bartolo with Konstantin Moskalenko (l), our veteran bass.

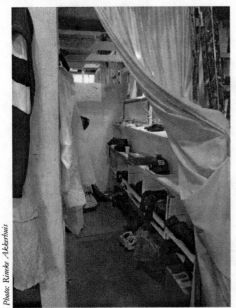

Photo: Rineke Akkerhuis

Chorus dressing room.

odd-looking traffic jam, which threatened to ruin a very delicate scene essential to the plot's development. There was only one possible thing to do to avoid potential embarrassment. As the girls continued to wind their way up to the stage, the last two geishas at the end of the line took the lady delicately by the arms and shoulders and escorted her to the door marked LADIES. They had no choice but to wait for her and help her back to her seat. By that time, the entrance chorus was not only over, but the onstage wedding ceremony was about to begin. They made a mad dash through the front door, around to the back of the theatre, through what was then a vast parking lot to the backstage exit to the dressing room and, as nonchalantly as possible, drifted gracefully onstage to join their geisha girlfriends. They managed to prevent what could have become a serious distraction in the aisle by their good deed and spontaneous thinking.

How it all worked was something of a miracle, but that miracle took place, I think, at least in part because our company functioned like a family, and everyone was there for everyone else. The adrenaline level was working overtime and the cast and crew were exhausted, but by the time the curtain came down, everyone was happily hugging one another.

Part of it had to do with the fact that our regular singers might be performing a small part in one opera and the lead in the next. It tended to make for a shared commitment onstage. Chorus members one night might be singing comprimario or leading roles the next night or later in the run, and they understood the demands of their colleagues' tasks. A majority of our company members had fulltime jobs during the week, and when most people were relaxing

Lit up and ready for showtime. The mural was painted by a young French boy who asked no fee except for the cost of the paint and the rental of a ladder. He wanted to show people of all races looking up at the Amato Opera sign. The mural brought us much attention, and the artist got many paying jobs as a result. Soon after, he disappeared and I can only assume he went back to France.

Photos: Laura Razzano

Three scenes of moving sets.

with the *New York Times* on the weekend, they made the choice to come in to the theatre to make a masterpiece like *The Marriage of Figaro* come alive time after time for over 100 audience members.

Once all the potential disasters were averted and the final curtain went down, that didn't mean we were finished with our responsibilities. If we were in the middle of a run, we would have to reset all the flats and props for the following night's rehearsal or performance before we called it a night.

If it was the end of the run, then it was quite another story. The last show was usually a Sunday matinee and, once it was over, the props and costumes all had to be brought back up to the top floors by means of the narrow, steep staircase, while the props and costumes for the coming opera about to go into rehearsal were all carried down the same four flights of stairs to the backstage area, employing as many as 40 volunteers to accomplish this task. In the meantime, huge flats and pieces of scenery were being hauled up and down the same flights of stairs in order to strike one production and get ready for the next one. It was strenuous, hard work, but great fun as well, and once we were all finished, everybody would sit down to a hearty meal of Tony and Sally's ziti and meatballs (of course, with a glass of red wine).

Finally, at the end of it all, it would be time for Sally and me to lock up the theatre and drag our feet to the nearby garage to start our 40-minute drive home. Sally would be half asleep by my side, but I could still hear her whispering, "Tony, you're crazy! A mad man!"

And that's what opera is all about!

Sally on the floor, eating with the kids after a show.

Part VII: New Projects

THERE is a familiar old saying about the two things that everyone can count on: death and taxes. Well, for an opera company, there are two additional things that are always true: 1) you always need more press, and 2) reporters don't come to cover standard repertoire. That meant that I had to keep thinking of new projects that would attract interest from the press.

Luckily, I always had a fascination with rarely-produced repertoire and I had collected a treasure trove of old scores down in the cellar. It was always a fun adventure for me to rummage around in old, lesser-known favorites or to find something entirely new as an inspiration for a production at the Bowery theatre.

A decision could never be made, though, as an intellectual exercise or on my preference alone. A choice of a new opera had to be made taking both artistic and business factors into consideration. I always found that focusing on production needs offsets other weaknesses—like high costs or an emotional tie to a score—that can get in the way when considering a new presentation.

I learned quickly to think very rationally about taking on a new production. My first thought would always be: "Are we equipped vocally—especially when it comes to the chorus—to bring out the merits of this particular opera?" People may find this surprising, since they might think that having the right tenor or soprano lead soloist is the biggest concern. But there are always capable people who are anxious for the opportunity to take on major roles. The hard part in a small company is finding the devoted regulars who will give their time for the less "glamorous" job of showing up night after night to carry the choruses and smaller parts.

The most important, and often-neglected, challenge of producing a mini-opera company for 60 years was the job of continuously putting on stage a happy and well-knit opera chorus. This was especially true with a volunteer chorus such as ours. My first task was to make sure I had a balanced group of voices in each category—soprano, mezzo-soprano, tenor, baritone, bass. My second task was to have a couple of people in each section who could read music and carry their section. The third major concern was to make sure that the people I chose would be consistent in attendance and faithful in learning their music. I had to explain these expectations carefully at the beginning of each season. Only then could I deal with the fourth issue—making a good visual picture; though I learned

Chorus, Scene I, Act IV, La Forza del Destino.

quickly how to cover up the problem of old people playing young parts and vice versa, and compensating for varying sizes of singers. Often I did this by creating character roles for the members of the ensemble. If, for example, one of my soprano chorus members looked a little too old to be a believable flower girl (remember, the audience was very close to the stage), I might give her the job of carrying on the water jugs during a particular scene and make her into a street vendor.

Working with a volunteer chorus is a matter of constant deal making. I had to make sure I had a chorus for every single performance. In order to do that, I'd promise my best ensemble singers roles in keeping with their abilities—as long as they would commit to the chorus when they weren't cast in larger roles. In general, this system worked well, because it rewarded the more experienced members, while showing the beginners that there was something to aim for. The result was excitement and satisfaction for both the veterans and the newcomers.

The actual work with the chorus required alot of patience on my part, but also created an artistic bond between me and my chorus members. We would start rehearsals with a little vocalizing and then I would have the chorus stand up and begin exercising with their bodies. Then we would sing a phrase or two of music, adding a few more bars when they were ready. Before they knew it, they would have their parts memorized. Once the music was pretty well learned, I would get them up on stage and start working on movement, so it would coordinate with the music. By the end of the rehearsal, I would always add, "You know you are getting salary for this job. I expect you to be well prepared by next week—or I'll hold back on your salary" (usually a whopping $5-$10 a show!).

Of course, the chorus is only one of the many different concerns that must be factored in and considered together as a whole when planning a new production: acting, singing, lighting, sets, orchestra, etc. But I am convinced that making sure, at the very beginning, that the production values were what they should be saved many of our operas and raised them to a level that met my standards. And that meant that I had to be sure I had the funds to make the show look right and that I could carry out each of the technical pieces of the puzzle in order to fulfill my vision of the opera I was considering.

This was not true in the old days, when opera just meant that people got up and sang. Back then, directors rarely had the opportunity to offer their ideas of the operas, since all that was provided was a piano rehearsal. At performance time, the person drawing the curtain (and often acting as the stage manager) would bark out from the wings: "Enter here! Sit there! Go there!" etc.—and that was it for stage direction. For me, good theatre meant combining all the parts into a complete and cohesive production, which I learned from my experience working in operettas and musical comedies.

Back when I was getting my start, people were often intrigued that I would accent all these production issues, because they weren't used to it. I learned some of my lessons very early on. One of my first experiences was directing a *La Traviata* in Syracuse with the soprano, Lucia Evangelista, who was perhaps better known as the wife of the famous Metropolitan Opera bass, Jerome Hines. Even though we had only limited resources to create stage effects, she still insisted that, in the death scene, the lighting be just right for the mood, and I realized what a difference this made. That was the first time I began to give serious thought to the importance of lighting in opera.

In considering new operas, I asked myself if I had all the talented people I needed to do the opera. Finally, I had to feel a connection to the dramatic possibilities of the story line. That's when I would start translating the score word for word, including all the indications in the score about stage directions, etc. This I would do before even beginning to learn the music.

Next, I would sit down with Richard Cerullo, who would immediately begin researching the historical background of the score to help me come up with a vision for the opera. We would plan the sets, always taking into consideration how we could economize by repurposing old flats and parts of previously-used sets, reworking them and adding new pieces we might need. I was always on the lookout for companies wanting to dispose of old scenery, and even television shows would call us up if they had costumes and props they wanted to get rid of.

We also developed a very loyal "grapevine." Through many ex-Amato artists who had moved on to loftier climes, we would get the "inside word" when the Metropolitan Opera was about to dump

Photo: Corinta Kotula

Our Merry Widow fountain was repurposed from Shelley Bartolini's whimsical version of Botticelli's "Venus on the Half Shell" from our very first La Traviata (Act II). Nathan Hull (l.) and Mark Bentley (r.)

old costumes, and we would be ready on a moment's notice to come with a van and pick them up. More than once, Sally answered the phone, only to hear, "Get up here now! You will find some great old costumes that are about to go out to the dumpster behind the theatre." This may sound like a small-time way to build up a company, but over the years, it enabled us to acquire a considerable supply of good quality materials that could be used as is or reworked for our own projects. And it gave us some history as well. Over the years, we came across costumes that had been made for Caruso, Richard Tucker, Lily Pons, Gladys Swarthout, and many other famous names. Former singers would also donate a career's-worth of personal treasure, including costumes, wigs, boots, etc. All of these became part of our own heritage—though not without Sally's genius with a safety pin, which saved many a day when it came to salvaging a costume that had seen many years of use.

My general rule, at the outset, was to allot each new show about $500 for new muslin, $250 for paint, and $500 for the fabric for costumes. I also would come up with a little extra salary for Richard's additional work. Rarely did a new production cost over $10,000, which would only happen in special cases when we had to start completely from scratch. And we would factor in our ability to use each new production over and over again as the years passed, not to mention pieces of sets, etc., that we could use in other productions. When we were lucky, a portion of the expense would come from contributions from our regular supporters.

One of the most enjoyable parts for me in planning new productions was collaborating so closely with Richard Cerullo, working together with him on each new scene as it was being painted, and discussing the historical background of what we were doing and where we were going next. Again, this was part of my belief that you learn new works as a whole, understanding the history along with the music when coming up with the correct architectural vision of a production that would work, not just as a musical score, but as a total theatre piece.

Once we had all the necessary pieces in place, I would be ready to start preparing for the new show, which I either scheduled after our summer break or after the mid-winter break, depending on our plans for the whole season and when we most needed the press coverage that we could count on for a new production.

Everything that I wanted to do with the staging was planned in advance, and it would all be marked up in my master score—from the major entrances and exits to important individual gestures that were necessary to convey the story, character, and action.

An annotated master score, ready for cast notes.

When you are working with, perhaps, six casts for a new show, this is not the time to "wing it" with stage directions. While the intricacies of stage business might be refined as we continued to work on the opera, it was essential that everyone come to rehearsal with the same basic building blocks already learned.

Then it would be time to cast the show. I knew the voices I had available each season with the company. In addition, twice each year, we would hold auditions. Over the course of one season, I would hear an average of 150 new singers. That meant that I had a good overall picture of the voices and talent I had available when planning the upcoming season. The ones that were chosen would be assigned solo parts or chorus participation.

All the cast members would then come in to the theatre and copy all the information from the master score and have one general musical reading, where I explained all the musical intricacies of the score. I would try to give the singers three to four months to learn their parts before holding musical and stage rehearsals. Very important to my system was to combine the music with the action so that everything would be learned together as a whole. Although my usual system was to offer only one stage rehearsal for standard opera productions, for new productions I was "generous" enough to have three stage rehearsals for each cast.

In order to achieve a cohesive visual opera production, whether it is a new show or standard repertoire, a director must insist from the cast that everybody has the same conception of the story line and one unified style of body movement, which is dictated by the music. For example, the style of movement appropriate to a verismo opera like *Cavalleria* would be totally inappropriate for a Mozart opera like *Don Giovanni*, even though both deal with the larger issues of seduction and betrayal.

I believe that this way of approaching a score is necessary for building a role as well as an opera. When some of the people who worked with me moved on to larger opera companies, they often came back to tell me that the training they received at the Amato Opera gave them the groundwork, even in big houses, when they were given little direction or perhaps none at all. With the base outline we had worked out, they could apply what they had already learned about their roles to less-than-ideal working situations. And, for me, the system allowed me to feel confident that the method would work even when faced with unfamiliar scores and new obstacles.

Not that the system was always the easiest for everybody to learn. Some of my singers found it very simple, but, for others, it took some time. My leading mezzo-soprano, Helen Van Time, for whom I have great admiration and respect for her love of the stage and also for her generosity to her colleagues and all the new, young singers she constantly helped with makeup and costuming crises, happens also to be very entertaining. Helen loves to tell the story of the dress rehearsal for her first big role with the company as Suzuki, Madama Butterfly's faithful servant.

Helen thought she could just learn her lines and follow Cio-Cio San around on stage, relying on sheer instinct. As Helen puts it, "to this day I still don't know how I, Tony, or Butterfly survived—mostly Tony." In a 6-hour rehearsal (*Butterfly* rehearsals usually lasted about half that time), Helen describes herself as having been "in a state of fascinating fright" as I had to demonstrate every single movement to her, pulling her around the stage to her proper positions.

*Rehearsing Helen Van Tine in the role of Marcellina (*Marriage of Figaro*).*

Helen made it through her performance that weekend, but I never took my eyes off her and made sure I could guide her to her proper positions on stage.

What is the point of this story? Well, two years later, she was singing a very exciting Amneris in *Aida*. She sang regularly with us ever after. Her delightful Mistress Quickly in *Falstaff* will always be stamped in my memory.

Helen was an example of a young artist who came to realize the importance of working in a disciplined manner, combining natural

Richard Cerullo's Nile Scene set for Aida.

Helen Van Tine and Mark Freiman in Aida.

instincts with a basic outline of the stage directions. Helen quickly moved to the Amato Opera director's staff and, in 1993, she directed a sensitive and exciting *Suor Angelica* for the company.

With Sally's help, she concocted 17 nuns' habits (raiding our *Trovatore* and *Forza* supplies), put together a cast of 17 women, and proceeded to discover how difficult it is to mount a production. When it was all over, Helen barricaded herself into a closet. Only Sally's offer of pasta and martinis finally got her to unlock the door.

Actually, she had done a very good job. I explained to her that if directors get back 10 percent of what they put into a show, then they should consider themselves lucky. After dealing with more-than-occasionally crazy singers, unprepared casts, and people who don't show up when you need them, it is doing one's own job to the best of one's ability that is what counts the most. It is something I often had to remind myself.

***

One of my earliest forays into new material came in 1953. By that time, we had already presented the popular double bill of *Cavalleria Rusticana* & *I Pagliacci* four times for a total of approximately 40 performances. It was a program that everybody loved, but I thought it would be interesting to pair something new with *I Pagliacci*. I had studied a number of Mascagni's scores, and found his little-known opera *Zanetto*. The play had been written by François Coppée in 1869 as a vehicle for the great Sarah Bernhardt. In it, she played the part of the boy Zanetto, a young troubadour who is seeking love. He encounters the beautiful and experienced Silvia, a courtesan from Florence. Instead of seducing him, Silva is so moved by Zanetto's innocence and goodness that she sends him on his way to discover true love. She finds, in the process, that her own cold heart has been awakened to love. Bernhardt played the role at a command performance for Emperor Napoleon III. Mascagni later saw the play performed by Eleanore Duse (again as the boy Zanetto), and he was inspired to write an opera on the subject.

Our production was well received. The *New York Herald Tribune* wrote that "The sets and general production were everywhere choice and elegant." The critics also liked the *Pagliacci* we paired it with. The *New York Times* particularly mentioned

> the ingenious and effective stage setting, which by opening doors and windows, transforms a traveling van into a theatre and thus does away with scene shifting.

One story particularly stands out in my mind about our 1953 *Zanetto.* I had felt so proud of myself for figuring out how to make a fountain for the first act garden scene set. I rigged up a garden hose from the backstage water supply on Bleecker Street and connected it to the stage fountain, where water issued forth from the mouth of a lion. Of course, it had another hose going out into the alleyway, where the water drained off. In those early days, we never

The infamous Bleeker Street Zanetto fountain.

thought about such a fancy solution to the problem as a motor, so we jerry-rigged everything we needed. I was quite pleased by the results.

The only problem was that, during performances, we discovered that any time anyone used the bathroom and flushed the toilet, the fountain would splutter and stop and then start spluttering again. First of all, we tried to forbid everyone from using the toilet during showtime. Then we posted a sign saying: BATHROOM OUT OF COMMISSION. Nothing worked. The only solution was to stop using the fountain completely, which was too bad, since it was a nice effect.

Luckily, I had learned my lesson when it came time, in 1973, to mount a new production of *Manon* at the Bowery theatre. It was the occasion of the company's 25th anniversary. What better way to celebrate than to surprise Sally with the revival of a new production of Massenet's *Manon* for her to star in. Sally's greatest talent was to make you feel that she was whatever role she portrayed, whether it

Sally and I — 25th Anniversary.

was Manon, Butterfly, Mimi, Violetta, etc., but many people especially loved her delicate portrayal of Massenet's heroine.

From our reading of the original Abbé Prevost novel, Sally and I both felt that the character of Manon was best captured by Massenet, as opposed to the Puccini version, which we never performed for that reason. But it also posed more problems for us, especially for the ensemble, because they were less familiar with French than Italian.

In the Act I scene of *Manon* that takes place in the square, we created a lovely fountain for the new production. This time, I made sure our budget allowed me to buy an electric circulating pump—something that we couldn't have even considered for the 1953 *Zanetto*. The pump re-circulated the same water (instead of the makeshift solution of spilling out into the alley). We incorporated the pump into the cutout of the fountain and the water poured through a spout onstage. There was a valve behind the set that controlled the flow. If it was not set correctly, the water would pour out too fast onto the stage, but even if it malfunctioned, Ricky was always there, alert to my frantic gestures, and he would dash behind the set to adjust the flow of the water, before nonchalantly coming back to continue the stage action.

Actually, we did a lot of learning on the spot from mistakes. Another famous one had to do with our snow machine at the Bleeker Street theatre. I concocted a three-sided track made out of chicken wire, which was turned by pulleys to release our falling snow—something particularly necessary in Act III of *La Boheme*. Not knowing what to use for snowflakes, I came up with the idea that oatmeal would make a good choice. The only problem was that, within a week, we had to make a drastic change, because the theatre became infested with well-fed mice backstage, who seemed to be thriving on their oatmeal diet. We quickly substituted confetti and the problem went away, since the mice didn't like the menu change.

Years later, in the Bowery theatre, when it came time to improve the production of our *La Boheme*, I made very good use of the construction skills of volunteer and good friend Eric Angelicola. Eric was in the construction business in New Jersey and he loved to sing, so he joined our ensemble and soon was singing assisting baritone roles. While he worked or was rehearsing onstage, his wife Fran would go upstairs to help Sally with the office work. To the very closing of the Bowery theatre, Eric was always willing to come in to help me with the annoying building problems that occasionally came up. Of the many things he tackled in the theatre, the first was figuring out what to do with our old snow track machine.

La Boheme calls for a lovely Parisian snowfall for the third act. Unfortunately, my old hand-made chicken-wire track made the "snow" come down all uneven. Sometimes it would stop dead, only to be followed by piles of snow that would dump onto the stage right in the middle of Mimi's third act aria—something my sopranos never much appreciated. After Eric rebuilt the machine, so it was now a closed tube with intermittent openings, the snow fell down in a much better-behaved fashion.

***

For our 1976 season, I wanted to do something special in honor of the United States bicentennial. I needed something that had a patriotic tone, and I decided to do a Verdi opera that had not been done before in this country—*La Battaglia di Legnano*. This opera had been written to a libretto by Salvatore Cammarano from a French play by Joseph Méry, *La Battaille de Toulouse*. The subject matter was patriotism and independence from foreign powers (not forgetting to include, of course, a tragic love triangle).

At the time the opera was written in 1848, Venice and Milan had just successfully revolted against their Austrian occupiers and there was a growing call for a new federation of the Italian republics. Verdi was looking to write on a subject that would showcase Italian nationalism, but could not forget that the censors had the power to stop productions of works considered too political. As a result, the story was transplanted to the time of Barbarossa in the 12th century. It didn't take much imagination, though, for audiences to know what was being suggested by the patriotic tale, especially since the fourth act is about the Milanese victory against the Austrians.

When *La Battaglia di Legnano* opened in Rome in January 1849, it was so well received that the ecstatic audience demanded that the entire fourth act be repeated from the very beginning! Even though the 1848 Italian "liberation" from the Austrians didn't last for long, and the opera was suppressed soon after when the Austrians regained power, it was one that Verdi had strong feelings about. He wrote: "Among my operas which are not in circulation, there are some I must forget about because their subjects were at fault. But I should like *La Battaglia di Legnano* not to be forgotten."

It seemed like the perfect opera about the joy of liberation for us to premiere at a time when America was celebrating its 200th year of freedom from the British. And it made me happy to think that Verdi himself might have approved our making this unknown work available to an American audience for the first time, 128 years after it had been written.

I decided to present the opera, not at the Bowery theatre, but in a location that would accentuate the theme of liberation. What better setting than New York's Cooper Union, where Abraham Lincoln had delivered his famous 1860 speech against slavery? Although the playing space was wide and narrow, Richard Cerullo and I thought we could make it work. Richard constructed a beautiful set that reflected the natural features of the hall, including its tall white col-

La Battaglia di Legnano *at Cooper Union.*

umns, to carry the sense of what was happening on stage out into the hall and we put considerable thought into how to make this spectacle come alive for our audiences.

The medieval-style costumes for *Battaglia* were executed by Sally and her new assistant, Ikuku Okaya, who was originally from Japan. Initially, Ikuku came to us to donate some lovely authentic kimonos for *Madama Butterfly*, but she decided to stay to help in the costume department. During a summer vacation in Italy, she brought back photos and pamphlets of the Lombardy region that we used as a resource in preparing *Battaglia*. Ikuku was a delightful person and a dynamo at the sewing machine. Unfortunately, her life was cut short in her mid-forties, the longterm consequence of radiation-related cancer from the bombing of Hiroshima in 1945. She was definitely missed by those who came to know her.

Our hard work on *La Battaglia di Legnano* was well-recognized by the critics. The *New York Post's* Harriet Johnson said:

> The opera was exciting . . . filled with juicy, stirring melodies. The overture is one of Verdi's best.

Opera News commented that

> Amato made the action, even when swashbuckling, believable. He conducted with conviction and an understanding of style as well as of his singers' needs.

The *Bergen Record's* Virginia Lambert called our production "remarkably good," and strongly suggested that

> [t]hose interested in Verdi opera should probably take advantage of these performances. There might not be a new production for another 128 years.

***

While all of this was going on, Sally had her own new projects. By the mid-'70s, we realized we desperately needed a new stage curtain. This was a major concern, because it was a big-expense item. It was also a particularly difficult curtain, because it didn't have the standard horizontal, side-to-side, opening that simply pulled the two sides apart. Instead, it was an Italian-style stage curtain that opened by looping up to the ceiling.

But the solution was one that our usual insanity dictated: Sally and Dolores Mari-Galdi simply decided they would make what we needed, even though they didn't have a clue how to do it. We were extremely lucky that a patron in the fabric business gave us two huge bolts of beautiful, pale-green silk brocade. I would have preferred another gold curtain, because our first one had been modeled on the Met's golden curtain, and we had hired a professional, at considerable expense, to make it for the opening of the theatre. This time, I couldn't beat the price (nothing is better than gratis!) and couldn't afford to be choosy. I also was able to recycle the old gold curtain as a mid-stage traveler curtain to be used to enclose fast onstage scene changes.

The sewing project took a great deal of nerve. With enormous trepidation, Sally and Dolores spread out the green fabric on the freshly-cleaned floor on the second level of the Bowery building. The next step was to take down the old gold curtain, carry it up to the second floor, and lay it out over the new fabric. They then marked all the dimensions and the places where there needed to be grommets for ropes. When tailor's chalk proved to be too light, they improvised, using black eyeliner. They then cut out pieces, panel by panel. Because they didn't know what they were doing, none of this was easy. Sally and Dolores were often joined by Mimi De Simone and Ann Carnevale, all sitting on the floor, holding their shears fearfully, until Sally would say, "Go ahead—just do it!" As they cut, Sally would sew together the four panels for each side of the curtain, breaking countless needles in the thick fabric.

The curtain took two weeks to cut and sew. It was definitely a labor of love. The sewing team laughed like crazy, fought like crazy, and miraculously got the job done. Now came the tough part of hanging it to see if they had done the job successfully. We all waited with bated breath, expecting the new curtain to collapse in a pile on the floor. It was a huge job. We had to put in all the rings and grommets and attach the ropes, not to mention weighting the hem with chains to make sure it had the proper swing when opened and closed. Finally, the moment came and I gave the order to pull the new curtain. As it swung open, we all gave a collective shout. It looked so beautiful!

Years later, in 2000, when we again needed a new curtain (even though Sally had carefully mended the green one for years), we returned to our gold-curtain tradition, only this time, it was electronically controlled and saved Sally alot of elbow grease pulling it by hand.

***

In 1978, I decided to do the U.S. premiere of Verdi's very first opera, *Oberto* (or *Oberto, Conte di San Bonifacio*), which he wrote when he was 26 years old. The plot is complicated, involving the defeated Oberto; his daughter Leonora, who has been raised without her parents by an old aunt; the tenor Riccardo, who seduced Leonora and is now marrying the mezzo-soprano Cuniza; public denunciations; and Oberto's challenge to fight a duel with Riccardo for his daughter's lost honor. The opera ends with Oberto's death in the duel, Riccardo's exile, and Leonora's despair.

I was reminded once again how lucky I was to have such a great painter as Richard Cerullo working with me. Unfortunately, Richard was out on a leave of absence when I wanted to do *Oberto*, so I employed a scenic designer with a great résumé from the Metropolitan Opera. On his very first day, he spent $500 on paint and brushes—my customary total for the entire production! For two weeks, he kept repainting—over and over—the first act set, never reaching a final decision on how it should look. There were times when I despaired, but the production eventually came off, although I must admit that I was disappointed with the visual aspect of the show.

Since I started this section talking about how necessary it is for a small company's survival to bring in the press, I am going to record here some of what was written about our productions. It's a little embarrassing to talk about all the good comments we received, so, believe me, I won't be insulted if readers want to skip some—or all—of the quotes from reviews that they will find on these pages. As Count Orlofsky tells us in *Die Fledermaus*, "Chacun a son gout"!

I must say that I was pleased at how often critics understood what the Amato Opera was all about. Yes, sometimes reviewers pointed out that the calibre of singing wasn't always even, but how else can a young artist learn the big operas for their future careers? Most of the critics didn't expect to hear the next Pavarotti at every performance, but that made it even more exciting when they did hear a great new singer in the making. If other cast members were not of the same level, they still were gaining desperately-needed training. Since I used up to six casts for each 12-performance run of an opera, there were always going to be some people who were more vocally prepared than others and people who had more stage experience alternating with newcomers. That was what my job as a teacher was all about.

Some critics thought we bit off operas too big for us to chew, but my point was to give the next Radames and Aida a place to begin to learn their roles, even if they might not be ready to do them on big stages for a few more years. The point was that we were doing something special at Amato Opera—and the positive comments from the critics who attended our productions not only kept new audiences coming to our shows, but also helped me to know that we were on track.

We were able to get some very good press for *Oberto*. H. Kupferberg wrote in the *Tribune*:

> I have just participated in an exhilarating musical adventure—the U.S. premiere of Giuseppe Verdi's first opera. In staging *Oberto*, Amato has scored a brilliant coup.

And Peter J. Rosenwald of the *Wall Street Journal*, writing about the production, noted:

> The Amato Opera theater is a tribute to the concept that opera can be good without being grand. For almost 30 years, Amato Opera has nourished young and enthusiastic opera buffs. . . .

Something that gave me particular pleasure during this production of *Oberto* was that my brother Albert came to New York from New London on weekends to play the piano for the show. Albert had lost his beloved wife Millie in December of 1975 and, although he was very busy managing the pharmacy, I like to think that he enjoyed filling some of his time by coming to the theatre. In July 1977, Albert got remarried to Zallee, his colleague at the drugstore.

Personally, I have such good memories of that time period. Sally and I would go to New London to visit Albert and Zallee, and it became our ritual to have a Sunday afternoon musical session, when I would take advantage of Albert's expertise at the piano to go over my newest music score. To feel and interpret the music when staging a new work, I would sing every single male and female role and chorus number from the beginning of the score to the very end. Albert would also coach Sally in whatever role she was currently preparing. Sometimes, my other brothers from New Haven would visit too, and we would all play and sing together, making the sessions memorable occasions.

By the end of these musicales, we would all be in a great, fun mood. Sally would sing some favorite Schubert lieder. When Zallee joined in, that topped it all as she would sing her heart out, with lots of interpretation, in her favorite art song. The absolute climax would come when Albert sang "Corteggiani" and "Nemico della patria" with tremendous fervor, voice cracking from emotion as he played and sang at the same time. Sometimes he could barely speak by the end, but tears of laughter came from all of us at the end of these impassioned impromptu musicales. It was a wonderful time of family and contentment.

Zallee began to come to New York when Albert played for our productions. Once she was truly a member of the family, I gave my "professional" opinion as to her future as a vocalist. My com-

ment was, "Zallee, an artist you will always be—a soprano, never."
After even that, she still loves me!

***

Our next new project, in 1979, was *La Cena delle Beffe* (*The Jesters' Feast*), the 1924 opera by Umberto Giordano (best known for *Andrea Chenier* and *Fedora*) and based on a popular play by Sem Benelli. The world premiere was at La Scala, conducted by Arturo Toscanini. Back in 1919, there had been a successful version of the play on Broadway, starring no less than John and Lionel Barrymore.

The story is, of course, terribly complicated—all having to do with the revenge one man takes on two brothers for stealing away his mistress. I like the summation of the plot that Peter G. Davis gave in his *New York Times* review of the production: "Set in late-15th-century Florence, the plot defies description, a veritable Renaissance orgy of lust, violence, blood feuds, revenge, intrigue, fratricide and madness." He went on to say about our production:

> The sets are especially attractive, admirably suggesting the work's decadent atmosphere. Anthony Amato conducted an ensemble of winds and piano, making every instrument count, a skillful compromise in lieu of a full orchestra. All the singers entered into the melodramatic spirit with gusto. . . .

I had more luck with the painting of the *Cena* sets than I did with the *Oberto* sets. Richard was still out on leave, but, as a special favor, my old friend Shelley Bartolino agreed to do the sets for the production. He was working in a big union scenic theatre shop on Long Island. I would bring the flats to him and, late at night, often after his work day was over, he painted our very complicated sets. The third act had a torture scene, and we set up a medieval rack. The hero was tied to a chair and brought up through the trap door. Chains came down from the ceiling and were attached to his wrists and ankles. In order to make him confess, he was tortured by turning the wheel to these chains. It was a very dramatic effect.

The apartment scene was very ingenious. Shelley painted a lusty nude onto a scrim. When the lights came up behind the scrim, you could see through the "wall" into the bedroom, where one of the two men out for revenge enters the room and seduces his brother's mistress while she is sleeping. It was really quite remarkable.

As often happens for me, thinking about the different productions we did reminds me of particular people and performances. For *La Cena delle Beffe*, I can't help remembering the baritone George Maldonado. From the beginning, George and I hit it off splendidly. He was an example of the fact that it is not always just the most magnificent voice that makes the best and most memorable performer. George's enormous love of singing, drama, and the stage were always an inspiration. He was extremely comfortable on the stage and he easily and gracefully shared his knowledge with young

Shelley Bartolino's torture chamber set for La Cena delle Beffe.

singers. He never was pushy about it, but, instead, he would gently guide novices and help them find their places on stage, explaining how a step or two to the left or a change in a stage angle would help a colleague or improve the overall picture for the audience.

In the case of *La Cena delle Beffe*, I very much enjoyed watching George's performance during the first act banquet scene. To heighten the effect, I decided to serve real food. How we did it was, just before the curtain went up, I took a whole chicken that had just been roasted upstairs on the second floor and placed it in the onstage "fireplace," where the electrical system was rigged so that the chicken would actually continuing warming while it was onstage, filling the theatre with the odor of roast chicken. Then, a servant would carry it on a platter to the principals. I remember how eloquently George would pick up the leg of the chicken and eat it in character—at the same time that he was singing and acting.

Unfortunately, George was taken away from us much earlier than he should have been. Even while he was waiting for a new kidney to prolong

George Maldonado (Rigoletto) and Patricia Sayre (Gilda) in Rigoletto.

his life, he continued to give fine performances for us. His exciting Iago in *Otello* and his extremely moving Rigoletto remain highlights for me of his performances.

***

In 1979, I decided to try another little-known opera, *Crispino e la Comare*, written in 1850 by two brothers, Luigi and Federico Ricci, with a text by Francesco Piave, better-known for the librettos he wrote for Verdi. There is a famous aria from the piece that Joan Sutherland recorded: "Io non sono piu l'Annetta." Once again, I liked Peter Davis's concise description of the plot in his *New York Times* review of the production:

> Crispino is a poor cobbler on the point of suicide because of unpaid debts, when his Comare, or fairy godmother, appears and sets him up as a fashionable doctor. After performing several miraculous cures, Crispino grows conceited, mistreats his wife, Annetta, and insults the Comare, who spirits him away to her underworld kingdom and shows the cobbler a vision of his own funeral. Cripino repents, and all ends happily.

I wanted to capture the lightness and fun of the opera and to make the text more accessible to the audience by presenting the opera in a bilingual English/Italian version. Luckily, I had exactly the right person to translate work on the English text for us: Lucy Weed. As I described earlier, Lucy wore many hats at the Amato Opera, and she would go on a few years later to

Crispino scolding his wife. Konstantin Moskalenko and Erika Nadir in Crispino e la Comare.

write the English translation of Boito's *Nerone* for us, as well as a performable version of Voltaire's drama, *Les Américains*.

Peter Davis liked the production, writing that "The Amato company did a remarkable job considering the limitations of its postage-stamp stage." He went on to say that my staging:

> caught the friendly, gentle wit of the piece admirably, and he exercised a firm hand over the musical proceedings. The production is a fairly elaborate one—there was even room to cram in a small stage band—and the modest but colorful sets were delightfully imaginative.

Speight Jenkins of the *New York Post* also liked what we did:

> Amato gives opera new life . . . a novelty of his current season and opera lovers should not miss it. It's a delightful comedy much in the style of Donizetti.

The *Daily News'* Bill Zakariasen noted:

Crispino e la Comare, *Town Square (Act I, scene 1)*.

The production (particularly the sets of Shelly Bartolini) was effective and the performance was enthusiastic.

Peter Wunne of the *Bergen Record* called it

> . . . a little known gem. Amato comes up with a rarity. It's funny and blessed with dozens of lovely singable melodies.

And the *Village Voice*'s Leighton Kerner called it

> . . . a comic fantasy: It has lots of catchy tunes and Anthony Amato's resourceful spirited production.

***

In 1981, I paired Mozart's early works, *Bastien et Bastienne* and *The Impressario* (using two strong and faithful members of the company, Victor Ziccardi and Trudy Wodinsky) for a delightful double bill. I was particularly happy that two of my leading singers, Deborah Surdi (soprano) and Kathy Enders (mezzo-soprano) participated as my assistant directors, as they did on many productions. As I've often mentioned, it always made me very happy when singers wanted to get involved in other areas of opera production.

The following year, 1982, Kathy Weyand, a lyric mezzo-soprano who sang a lovely Cherubino for me, suggested a double-bill of Hindemith's *Hin und Zuruck* and Stravinsky's *Mavra*. I found the idea very appealing. From my Bleeker Street days, I always felt it was important not to be known only as a Verdi/Puccini man, and my forays into other composers gave me quite alot of courage.

Kathy also helped me a few years later, in 1985, when she directed another lesser-known opera, Massenet's *Thérèse*, which is a sad story about a love-torn maiden during the French Revolution. That same year, I did an interesting double bill, Verdi's eighth opera, *Alzira*, coupled with the Voltaire drama, *Les Américains*, upon which the opera is based. Lucy Weed's English version of the play worked well for us, and I liked doing a play along with the opera for a change

Richard Cerullo and I working on the Alzira *sets.*

of pace and to show the differences between the two; although, I must say, the plots of both may not be considered particularly memorable.

The action takes place in Peru and deals with the power struggle between the native Indians and the conquering Spanish. Naturally, it involves the usual unhappy love triangle between the Indian maiden Alzira, her beloved Zamoro, and a

Sally and I clowning around on a new set for Alzira.

forced marriage to Guzman, the son of the Spanish governor. It ends with Zamoro killing Guzman, Guzman's Christian pardoning of his murderer, and a recognition by all parties of Christian mercy. The opera does provide some exciting music in the early Verdi style, and it did give Richard Cerullo the opportunity to come up with some wonderful, exotic sets.

***

When it came time for the company's 35th anniversary in 1983, I decided to take on a huge project, the first U.S. full-staged production of Boito's *Nerone*. While never a standard, Arrigo Boito's first opera, *Mefistofele*, had its fans (remember how surprised I was when my close friend Frank Szymanski announced that it was his favorite opera). Even fewer people knew about Boito's second, and last, opera, *Nerone*—an amazingly complex story of the Emperor Nero, his guilt over his murder of his mother, and the battle between paganism and Christianity in Rome, complete with a vestal

Richard Cerullo's sketch of the Act III set for Boito's Nerone.

virgin in love with the leader of the Christians and a snake-charmer lady in love with Nero.

You can't say the opera doesn't try for big effects, since it includes Simon Magus thrown from the top of a tower (to prove his claim that he can fly), and the opera culminates with nothing less than the burning of Rome, except that in this operatic version of the historical event, the fire was set to rescue the Christians imprisoned by Nero.

Boito had started and fully intended completing a fifth act. This last scene takes place in Nerone's private theatre, where the emperor's own version of the Orestiad (the classic story about killing one's mother) is about to be played. While this scene was not totally completed before Boito's death, extensive notes and sketches existed. I thought it would make a better ending than stopping at the end of the previous scene, which is the more common way of presenting the opera. In my research, I found some of the composer's original sketches and I was inspired, in my own humble way, to put together a musical drama to complete what had originally been part of Boito's vision of the opera.

In order for the audience to have some idea about the strange goings on in this opera, I decided to do *Nerone* in English. As she had done before for *Crispino e la Comare*, the extremely talented Lucy Weed wrote the English translation for us.

There were plenty of problems in producing *Nerone*. First of all, it was very difficult to cast. While much of the music is very beautiful, it also requires quite a bit of virtuoso singing. I also knew that I wanted the burning of Rome to be rather monumental, not the easiest effect to show on stage. It took the purchase of an additional five fog machines. Hoses from the machines came out of the perches, the wings, and the balcony, and they spewed fog out all over the stage and part of the theatre. We had to make sure that the exhaust system was always working properly, because it had to draw out all the fog at the climax, when hundreds of pieces of styrofoam, representing buildings, fell from the ceiling. At every performance, I had to have 10-12 people working the ropes that overturned the boxes on the ceiling, allowing the styrofoam "rocks" to pour down onto the stage.

Another challenge was how to stage the scene in which Nerone taunts Simon Magus. We had an extension ladder hanging on the side wall by the orchestra seats. When Nero orders Simon to prove he can "fly," the ladder was placed in the orchestra pit, leaning up against the balcony. With the soldiers prodding Simon with their spears and the chorus of 40 people singing onstage, Simon climbed above the audience and over the balcony rail to disappear into the darkness, while the chorus pantomimed his falling to his death at the climactic section of the music, complete with loud screams. It was quite an effect!

All our work paid off well, given the enthusiastic response in

Nerone, *Act IV.*

the press. The *New York Times'* Tim Page said:

> we must be grateful to the Amato Opera for bringing [*Nerone*]
> to New York. . . . The Amato Opera's small but spirited pro-
> duction will not likely be surpassed for quite some time.

Bill Zakaraisen, in the *New York Daily News*, wrote:

> Opera in top visual & vocal form: Vocalism and production
> hold their own with Amato's *Nerone*, in which artistic direc-
> tor Anthony Amato has attempted to flesh out Boito's un-
> finished last act's sketches. Amato has done an amazing job
> with the C.B. DeMille action of the story . . . tigerishly bring-
> ing it right into the audience when the stage can no longer
> accommodate all of it. . . . The sets are absolute knockouts
> in impressiveness and authenticity.

Peter Davis was equally complimentary in *New York Magazine*:

> I'm not sure why the Amato Opera production of Boito's
> *Nerone* worked as well as it did; perhaps it was the appealing
> David-versus-Goliath spirit that spurred everyone involved.
> Even the Met would be overtaxed by this behemoth. . . .
> Richard Cerullo successfully extended his elaborately de-
> tailed sets along the walls of the auditorium, vestal virgins
> capered gamely down the center aisle, and director Anthony
> Amato used every inch of space with remarkable ingenuity.
> . . . Amato Opera's heroic efforts did give New York its
> first, and probably last, chance to see this legendary example
> of operatic hubris on stage.

As usual, Andrew Porter offered thoughtful comments in *The New
Yorker*:

> Nerone, richly and skillfully designed by Richard Cerullo,
> was impressive. Spectacle is partly a matter of proportion.
> This show had a cast of seventy, pouring on to pack every
> inch of the theatre in the first-act finale. To achieve a com-
> parable cast-to-audience ratio, a Met *Nerone* would need a
> cast of well over two thousand. . . . The piece was sung in a
> well-fashioned English translation by Lucy Weed. . . . An-

thony Amato included a presentation of the uncomposed final act, one of the strangest scenes in opera, while Rome blazes to destruction all around . . . and it is needed to bring Boito's astounding drama of history and myth, actuality and illusion, eroticism and religious passions, philosophy and psychology to its resolution.

I can't say that getting reviews like that is what it's all about, but recognition in the press goes a long way in making you feel that you are on the right track—not to mention the increased ticket demand after the critics take positive notice of a production.

***

In 1984, we produced the charming Donizetti one-act opera, *Il Campanello di Notte* (*The Night Bell*). The story was great fun for the audience, as it is a story of one man's attempt (wearing various disguises) to keep his ex-mistress from the arms of her aged husband on their wedding night. Elizabeth Hastings conducted and directed the staging. Liz was one of my only pianists who took an interest in getting involved in staging. She also taught me to be neat in making notes in my scores, since her own notes are so tidy. She is a wonderfully accomplished artist; to this day, when she coaches singers in an opera, she sings all the other parts while she is playing. If she was working with someone who was preparing for one of my productions, she also gave them my staging—all read from her meticulous notes at the same time she was playing the piano.

With Elizabeth Hastings and Nathan Bahny at their wedding. Metropolitan Opera tenor Nico Castel (who officiated) is at right: He sang the Count in Barber of Seville *with us at the very beginning of his career.*

I was lucky to have Liz working with me for a number of years, and she was also responsible for directing *Dr. Miracle*, which we did in 1986. In return, the Amato Opera can take credit for introducing Liz to Nathan Bahny, a lyric baritone who could learn a role on the spot. In a world of constantly shifting romantic pairings, they have proven to be a devoted and happy couple and it was a great pleasure for me to walk Liz down the aisle at their wedding.

***

The search for something novel and interesting that will merit press coverage never ceases. Looking through scores to find another project, I came across the works of Brazilian-born composer, Antonio Carlos Gomes (1836-1896), author of 11 operas. I was struck by the Verdian quality of his writing and began to learn more about him. I certainly was impressed when I discovered that Verdi called Gomes "a true musical genius."

Gomes was born in Campinas, Brazil, the 11th child (in a family of 26) of his provincial bandmaster father. It was his father who taught him music and made sure his son mastered several instruments. After studying at the conservatory in Rio di Janeiro, he

Sally in a Mostly Gomes sweatshirt.

wrote two operas. His second won him a grant to study in Italy, where his work was noted positively by Verdi himself.

Since Gomes' operas were relatively unknown in the United States (even though they continue to be performed in Brazil—especially his most popular work, *I Guarany*)—and I was intrigued by both the music and the plots of his operas, I decided to present his work at the Amato Opera. For the 1986-1987 season, we produced the first opera, *Salvator Rosa*, in what would end up being a series of three: *Salvator Rosa*, *Lo Schiavo*, and *Fosca*. Taking a playful jibe at New York's renowned Mostly Mozart summer festival, we took to calling our own season, "Mostly Gomes."

Salvator Rosa, written in 1874 to a libretto by Antonio Ghislanzoni (who wrote the libretto for Verdi's *Aida*) is set in 17th-century Naples and concerns the 1647 Neopolitan rebellion against the occupying Spanish. Rosa, historically a famous artist/musician of the time specializing in battle-scene paintings, is known to have participated in the insurrection. In this opera, when Rosa is captured by the Duke of Arcos, the woman he loves, Isabella (who happens to be the duke's daughter) ransoms him by promising to marry one of the hated Spaniards. At the end, rather than choosing this fate worse than death, Isabella chooses the latter and poisons herself, but not before all the characters call for freedom, patriotism, peace, and reconciliation—all of which bring early Verdi operas strongly to mind.

Working with Richard Cerullo on sets for Salvator Rosa.

Richard Cerullo's artist studio set for Salvator Rosa, *showing some of Rosa's actual paintings on the right and left sides of this photo.*

One of Richard Cerullo's original sketches for Salvator Rosa *sets.*

Richard Cerullo designed wonderful sets for the production. Because Rosa was a noted artist, Richard even incorporated some of his actual paintings into the artist studio set of Act I.

I got my wish when it came to press coverage. Neither Richard Cerullo nor I had any reason to be dissatisfied by what the critics had to say. *New York Magazine*'s Peter C. Davis commented that

> no true connoisseur of operatic arcana will want to miss the Amato Opera's full production of *Salvator Rosa* . . . the work gives a good idea of what [Verdi] admired. Gomes animates each scene with music of a very specific dramatic character; he respects conventional forms but handles them imaginatively; and, above all, he keeps everything moving briskly. . . . Richard Cerullo's colorful, tastefully executed sets and costumes set off the opera handsomely. . . . Of course, what makes it all work—and what has made the Amato such an endearing community institution over the past 40 years—is its founder, conductor, and stage director, Anthony Amato, whose irrepressible enthusiasm for putting on opera is as infectious today as it ever was.

The *New Yorker*'s Andrew Porter compared the plot of the opera to a cross between Verdi's *I Vespri Siciliani* and Puccini's *Tosca*, and added that

> Gomes was a fluent and able composer, and there were no dull patches in the work. . . . Anthony Amato, musical and stage director, works wonders in recreating the effects of grand opera with small resources. His sense of dramatic timing is sure. Richard Cerullo has designed and painted seven picturesque and appropriate sets.

He was not the only one impressed by what Richard had done. *Newsday*'s Peter Goodman said that

> The sets and costumes, by Richard Cerullo, were exceptional, offering scenes from a Romanesque cloister to a busy harbor marketplace rich with detail and color.

The *New York Daily News*'s Bill Zakariasen mentioned that

> This presentation . . . certainly looks magnificent, thanks
> largely to Richard Cerullo's superb period sets. . . . *Salvator
> Rosa* is worth any opera buff's time.

The *New York Times* (Michael Kimmelman) said that

> Richard Cerullo has done magic with the sets, evoking a
> series of large-scale scenes on the very small stage.

Anthony D. Coggi ("The Operaphile") commented on WFUV-FM
radio:

> Much of the evening's success was due to Richard Cerullo's
> extremely handsome costumes, and seven sets which man-
> aged to infuse a sense of opulence, airiness and space on
> the theatre's minuscule stage. They are among the most at-
> tractive and apt I've seen anywhere this season (and that
> includes Lincoln Center!). Last but not least, praise to the
> indefatigable and dynamic 'Karajan of the Bowery,' mae-
> stro Anthony Amato, who, as usual, staged as well as con-
> ducted. If but half his energy and talent could be harnessed
> and somehow injected onto some of the other impresarios
> and conductors around town, New York's operatic life would
> be that much more lively.

Not only did the more familiar newspapers want to see what
we were doing, but so did the Hispanic press. Peter Bloch, writing
for *Canales*, the only major magazine catering to the Latino community at the time, had this to say:

> The work requires elaborate staging, and this was indeed
> provided by the Amato Opera. Its pretty theater is small,
> but the sets, costumes and choruses rank with those of the
> best opera houses and are superior to those of some pro-
> ductions I have seen at the Met and the N.Y. City Opera. It
> is marvelous what Anthony Amato, Sally Amato and Rich-
> ard Cerullo (scenery and costumes) have wrought. . . . Since
> 1948 no one is doing more for the cause of opera in New
> York than Maestro Amato, who has presented quite a few

unjustly neglected masterworks and is a superb musician able to generate excitement even with a very small orchestra, as well as a remarkably gifted stage director. It is obvious that he also knows how to find and develop the right singers.

We repeated a series of performances of *Salvator Rosa* the following year and then, in 1988, given the extent of the positive reaction, I decided to do another Gomes opera, *Lo Schiavo,* which dealt with the issue of freedom from oppression.

I decided to present the opera at Marymount College instead of at the Bowery theatre, to allow for a more monumental production, taking advantage of Marymount's large auditorium, which could seat about 800 people, and permitting me to use a much-expanded orchestra.

At the time Gomes began working on *Lo Schiavo,* slavery still existed in Brazil. In fact, it was not abolished there until 1888—one year before the premiere of Gomes' opera.

The Countess's reception room, Lo Schiavo, *Act II.*

Gomes originally used a Portuguese libretto written by his friend, the Viscount of Taunay, to tackle this work about Brazilian slavery. However, the Italian librettist and translator, Paravicini, insisted on making changes to satisfy operatic conventions (and, no doubt, the censors!) and the date of the action was moved back to the 16th century. The black slaves were changed to native Indians, and the Portuguese noblewoman of the original plot was changed to a French countess. No one in Brazil would have doubted the subject matter however; even though, by the time the opera opened in Rio di Janeiro in 1889, slavery had been abolished the previous year. For our own production, I restored the story to its original subject matter.

The plot revolves around a love story between a slave (Ilara) and Americo, the son of the slave master, Count Rodrigo. To break up their attachment, the Count sends Americo off to the army to

(l. to r.) Joe Pariso, Lynn Dolce, and Vincent Titone in Lo Schiavo.

fight against the slaves' uprising. He forces Ilara to marry another slave, Ibere (the slave of the opera's title), despite Ilara's declaration of undying fidelity to Americo. Of course, the story would not be complete without a noblewoman who is also in love with Americo. A great deal is said about slavery, there is plenty of torture and misery, and there are innumerable misunderstandings before the opera ends with Ibere's self-sacrifice so that the two lovers can be together.

The *Daily News* (Bill Zakariasen) called the work "A Buried Treasure" and noted that in *Lo Schiavo*

> late Verdi is perfectly balanced with the newer verismo school—albeit with a far greater command of ensemble numbers than any other verismo composer was capable of in 1889.

He added that

> Anthony Amato's conducting and staging kept the opera excitingly alive, Richard Cerullo's designs were convincing, and the cast . . . delivered the goods robustly, and so did the chorus.

The *New York Times* (Will Crutchfield) also found the work intriguing, saying

> A younger, less demanding Verdi could have set the libretto himself, and might not have been ashamed of the sweeping massed ensembles and lyrical solos that Gomes produced. Engage Placido Domingo, Aprile Millo and Giorgio Zancanaro with somebody like Giuseppe Patane to conduct and you'd have a hot night at the Met.

Looking at the photos of *Lo Schiavo* makes this a good time to mention Vincent Titone, the Amato Opera's leading veteran tenor. Since his debut in *Faust* in 1970 and right through the very last year of Amato Opera productions in 2009, Vincent has sung over 700 opera performances of leading tenor roles with us. His caressing vocal phrases, along with his chiaroscuro technique, have always been an inspiration for me to keep on singing myself. With his musical background and talent, Vincent will make an ideal vocal coach. Not that all of this came to him by a direct route. Vinny was originally studying for a doctorate in psychology and he worked for a time as a school psychologist. But a person's true path can't be kept in hiding forever. He decided to give up the endless paperwork of a school psychologist's life, and he switched careers and became a church music director, where, in addition to his singing, he also played the organ.

Another very good and reliable member of the company is Joe Pariso. From the very first day he came to the theatre as a chorus member, he helped making sets and loading and unloading scenery. Soon he moved into comprimario and then leading baritone roles. Unfortunately for me, this arrangement didn't last long, because he got married and had to get better jobs—something I certainly understood from my own life. Joe was accepted into the Metropolitan Opera chorus, where he went on to take assisting roles. In 1998, he and Sally collaborated on directing Wolf-Ferrari's *Secret of Susannah*. Until the very end of the Bowery theatre, if Joe had a free day when we were striking a set, he would still come back to help. He is a truly decent and open-hearted man.

***

In 1996, I took the opportunity to round out my Gomes productions with a third, *Fosca*. For this opera, Gomes took the action to Istria and Venice in the mid-15th century. It involves pirates, the Venetian Doge, a pirate woman (Fosca) and a Venetian lady (Delia) both in love with the same Venetian captain (Paolo). There is a lot of talk of ransom and battles and a dose of poison that gets passed between the women. The opera suitably ends with Fosca's death and the pirates' call for vengeance against Venice.

The review in *New York Magazine* predicted that Gomes would eventually be considered "little more than an interesting bridge between Verdi and Puccini." All the same, the review added that

> Still, it was good to be exposed to the piece this once, and the Amato production worked its usual miracle of achieving scenic grandeur (sets by Richard Cerullo), theatrical panache, and a big musical spirit with the most modest resources.

***

Besides our Gomes series, I did a number of other new productions during the same time period. One of these new shows brings to mind a very funny story concerning Eric Angelicola, whom I've mentioned before for building us a new snow machine for the Bowery theatre.

Knowing I could count on Eric since he was so attentive to details, I gave him important duties to perform during a complicated scene change I devised for a new *Ballo in Maschera* that we did in 1989. I decided to use a blackout in order to allow the witch Ulrica's magic smoking cauldron to emerge in the darkness from the trap door into position on stage. For this to happen, in

Un Ballo in Maschera, *gallows scene.*

Un Ballo in Maschera, *last act opera house.*

full view of the audience, all my staff on stage had to do double duty to make this somewhat elaborate procedure work properly.

On opening night, in his excitement, Eric fell directly into the cauldron as it was ascending to stage level. While the whole audience was watching the spectacle in the flickering firelight, Eric's head could be seen sticking up from inside the huge pot, where he added to the unusual effect by coughing and choking from the thick fog that came up from the depths of the cauldron. This certainly added some interesting ideas about what the witch Ulrica was busy cooking up in her cauldron! But none of this fazed Eric, who just hoisted himself up and out and hurled himself back on stage, with only a few scratches to show for his ordeal. At intermission, he just shrugged and commented, "The show must go on!"

Later, when we repeated the production in 1996, we received a lovely review from an Australian publication, *Opera Australasia*, whose critic, David Gyger said the following:

> When chorus time rolled round, the ingenuity of the Amato exercise was quite astonishing—faces popped out from every conceivable nook and cranny of the proscenium wall; elbow to elbow and cheek by jowl, they dwarfed their stage environment inevitably seeming themselves larger than life. But the illusion was virtually complete: never have I spent a more fascinatingly rewarding session at the opera than this.

His review continued:

> When next your globe-trotting gene takes you to the Big
> Apple, you could do far worse than seek out a performance
> at Amato Opera. Much worse.

Another rarity that I staged in 1990 was Verdi's early opera, *I Due Foscari*, based on a play by Lord Byron. *Opera Monthly* very succinctly described the plot as follows:

> It shows the dark side of Venice and the dreaded influence
> of the powerful Council of Ten who destroy the lives of
> Francesco Foscari, Doge of Venice, and his son Jacopo.

The critic went on to say:

> One would assume it was presumptuous of the minor league
> Amato Opera to stage this extremely difficult opera but, in
> the event, they succeeded admirably. In a tiny theatre that
> seats only 107 people and an orchestra of maybe eight musicians, they gave a very convincing and enjoyable performance of Verdi's flawed but still vastly impressive work.

I Due Foscari, *showing the Venetian canal in the background.*

The *New Yorker*'s Andrew Porter wrote:

> Anthony Amato, the conductor and stage director, and Richard Cerullo, the designer, worked once again their accustomed miracle: they brought a grand opera to life with very modest solo, choral, instrumental, and scenic resources. Confidence and a sure feeling for style play a large part in it.

***

In 1992, the 500 year anniversary of Christopher Columbus's discovery of America called for something special.

Since the 1985-86 season, we had been lucky to have the composer, pianist, and conductor Tim Mallard working with us. Over the 10 years he spent with the company, he produced a number of interesting presentations for us, including a memorable one using famous opera passages to demonstrate the compositional techniques of Leonard Bernstein and Aaron Copland. Even though he worked full-time at JFK airport and gave piano lessons in students' homes, he still took the time to write a special cantata for the 500-year celebration of the discovery of the New World. Tim, who is the most modest of talented men, reacted with surprise when I asked him to write a piece for us. As he put it: "Feeling honored, challenged, and as if I had nothing to lose, I said of course, I would love to give it a try."

We decided to use Christopher Columbus's own words, which had been recently translated into English, to create a semi-staged cantata called *Profecias* that could be described as a semi-staged oratorio. An undercurrent of diverse musical styles recreated a voyage from the Old World to the New and the apocalyptic fourth movement represented Columbus's vision for the end of the world as well as the actual apocalypse faced by the native peoples whose civilizations were eventually destroyed by their encounter with Europeans.

The premiere of *Profecias* was a bit later than originally planned, in August of 1992, due to an accident that Tim had. He ended up conducting the piece with a huge cast on his leg.

Sightlines reviewer Iris Bass pointed out in her review that

> *Profecias* is not quite an opera, but a heavily-atmospheric ora-
> torio calling for a 'trinity' of soloists plus a baker's dozen
> chorus of 'apostles' and, at the very end, a child soprano,
> who were all set here against one of set designer Richard
> Cerullo's beautiful backdrops. . . .

Profecias garnered a nomination for an award from the American Academy of Arts and Letters, and Tim also received a grant
from the "Meet the Composer" program of the NEA. In Tim's
characteristically humble manner, he credits the support and interest
of his wife, soprano Deborah Goin, for his success.

***

The following year, 1993, I finally was able to stage Verdi's
Otello for the first and only set of performances at the Amato Opera. While I had long wished to do *Otello*, the notorious difficulty of
casting the tenor lead had held me back for a long time. Because the
story was from Shakespeare, I did the production in English.

The press hinted that the opera was out of our range and
that we should concentrate our efforts on smaller pieces. However,

IV Act bedroom set, Otello.

Act I Otello, *from the right perch.*

James Landers (Otello) and Rebecca Sieglar (Desdemona) in Otello.

except for the Act II finale and the opening storm scene, I considered it to be an intimate opera.

During that first scene, I had Ricky running around like a madman creating the thunder effects. Then he was in charge of making the ships toss in the storm. We did this by using cutouts of ships in different sizes to give perspective and give the sense of the expanse of the ocean. Ricky had to rock the individual boats back and forth by means of rods attached to the cutouts, conveying an excellent impression of a storm-tossed sea.

The photos of the production bring to mind our lead soprano Rebecca Sieglar, who sang so many of the more dramatic roles for us. In addition, in later years, Rebecca took charge of the wig department, where she lovingly tended the multitude of wigs we needed for every production. One night she would wear the soprano heroine's long-tressed wig to sing, but she would be back the next night to make sure the same wig looked good on the next soprano. Often, just before a crucial entrance, there would be Rebecca, comb in hand, patting a final curl into place before the singer hurled him- or herself onstage to sing.

There are so many wonderful people who worked with us during this time. One I would like to mention is Knighten Smit, who assisted in many departments of our productions, and who produced a presentation of Bartok's *Bluebeard's Castle* for our Guild in 1995. Knighten, who later became a director at the Metropolitan Opera, worked with me for about three years, where he also shared his expertise in building sets and writing press releases. I made sure to reward him as much as possible with something he truly loved—my pasta!

***

In 1997 I took the opportunity to indulge myself by going back to my favorite opera—Verdi's *Falstaff*. I've always believed that Verdi was a master at making Shakespeare's words come to life. The opera was difficult to conduct with all its complicated musical cues, but there is a pattern to it all, and once you understand that structure, everything seems to fit together like a jigsaw puzzle. Because I always think of performance problems as a whole, I came up with a method that helped tremendously in staging the notoriously difficult last act fugue. It is a scene that singers (and conductors) worry a great deal about, because the musical entrances are very difficult. What I did was to arrange the characters on stage in the order in which they sing, making it less nerve-wracking for the singers, and allowing me to give cues just by moving down the line, rather than wasting time you don't have at that point searching for the character who needs to sing next.

After studying and producing *Falstaff* over the years, I have

Searching for Falstaff, Act II.

Falstaff: *(l. to. r.) Robert Shaffer (Bardolfo), Garth Taylor (Falstaff), Marc Berman (Pistola).*

come to believe that there isn't a single note in the score that fails to tell me something about the action. I was lucky in that the singers who studied with me learned to approach the opera from a dramatic point of view. I found this to be particularly necessary in *Falstaff*. The casting requires good actors, people with good musicality and timing, not to mention a strong sense of ensemble performance. For me, there is no question that *Falstaff* is an ensemble opera. If anyone needs an example to prove this, then the reading of the two love letters in Act II, scene 1 is a perfect case in point to demonstrate Verdi's beautiful legato flow.

There was a magical scene change that we used in *Falstaff* that always brought down the house. After the Garter Inn scene (Act II, scene 1) comes the transition to the forest scene. The way we did it was to have a magic tree arise. The trunk of the tree was a tube rolled up behind a barrel, controlled by a pole in the pit. When the pole came up through a hole in the floor of the stage, it entered into the base of the rolled-up tube and, as it was pushed up, the trunk sprang to life. At the same time, the foliage for the top of the tree descended from the ceiling to meet the rising trunk.

While all of this was going on, the walls of the inn from the previous scene reversed to reveal a forest, and the panorama of the sky also turned into a forest of trees by means of a drop. All of this was done while the French horns played the call for the hunt to begin that opens the scene. Then, finally, as the moonlight began to play over the forest, the audience watched the clouds part and were able to experience all the magic of this scene as Fenton enters, serenading his beloved Nanetta.

***

At the time, it seemed almost impossible to believe that so many years had flown by, but 1998 was the 50th anniversary of the

Amato Opera. It was a busy year, and one in which I added a production of Mascagni's *L'Amico Fritz* to accompany *I Pagliacci*. I had always wanted to do that work, since I found it, after *Cavalleria Rusticana*, to be the most original of Mascagni's operas. I had spent quite a bit of time studying Mascagni scores, but, too often, I found that the orchestral interludes were too long, so they interfered with building a dramatic climax. That being said, as a singer, I loved Mascagni's tenor arias!

Our 50th anniversary was the occasion for a grand celebration at the Baroque Room of the Plaza Hotel. It felt like everyone was there, including Licia Albanese and Mignon Dunn. Neil Shicoff

was in Europe and couldn't join us, but he sent two dozen red roses that we proudly displayed on the grand piano. Past and present singers joined in for a wonderful event that included, of course, lots of singing. I even got to serenade Sally!

We were very honored to receive special greetings from President Bill Clinton and New York's Mayor Rudolph W. Giuliani. Mayor

Serenading Sally at our 50th anniversary celebration at the Plaza Hotel.

Sally and I at the Plaza for the 50th Anniversary celebration, 1998.

Giuliani (like Mayors Koch and Wagner before him), when his schedule permitted, came to see productions at the theatre, and he used an
interesting publicity shot with our cast of *Tosca* to illustrate a feature
article about himself in *The New York Times.*

***

Amato: A Love Affair with Opera, produced and directed by
Stephen Ives and shown on PBS, gave the Amato Opera international recognition.

Ives lived nearby and was curious about what was going on at
the theatre. He came to see a number of shows and, after we chat-
ted a bit, we really took to each other and soon became inseparable.
It didn't take long for him to become obsessed with the idea of
helping the Amato Opera. He decided to do a documentary, even
though he had a busy schedule of paid jobs, including a well-known
documentary he did on the American West. But, whenever he had a

(from left) Licia Albanese, me, Sally, and Mignon Dunn at our 50th Anniversary celebration.

NY City Mayor Giuliani on a visit to the Bowery theatre.

THE WHITE HOUSE
WASHINGTON

October 29, 1997

Warm greetings to everyone celebrating the 50th anniversary
of the Amato Opera Company.

The Amato Opera Company has delighted music lovers throughout the years, establishing an extraordinary artistic tradition
in New York City. You can be proud of the outstanding talent
of your artists and the success of your productions.

I applaud the management, staff, performers, musicians,
volunteers, and supporters of the Amato Opera Company for
broadening the appeal and reach of this unique art form.
Thanks to your efforts, generations of appreciative fans have
been entertained and inspired, and I am confident that the
Amato Opera Company will continue to enhance New York's
cultural life for many years to come.

Best wishes for a memorable anniversary season and
continued success.

Bill Clinton

THE CITY OF NEW YORK
OFFICE OF THE MAYOR
NEW YORK, N.Y. 10007

May 17, 1998

Dear Friends:

It is with great pleasure that I send my warmest greetings to those attending
today's luncheon. This is a special occasion as you celebrate the 50th season of the
Amato Opera Theatre.

On behalf of the residents of New York City I congratulate Tony and Sally Amato
for reaching this important milestone. Over the past fifty years they have brightened
and enlightened the lives of New Yorkers of all ages to the wonders of opera. I applaud
them for the energy, enthusiasm and passion they have put into every single one of
their performances since their first production of "Barber of Seville" in 1948. In addition
I commend them for encouraging young opera singers to follow their hearts and to
pursue roles that have very often lead to great and world-renowned careers.

The Amato Opera Theatre is a truly extraordinary New York cultural institution
and it is a priceless addition to our great City's music industry. I salute the members of
the Amato Opera Theatre for teaching opera to school children through a variety of
unique and creative programs. As all those associated with the Amato Opera Theatre
look back on their glorious past, I wish them the very best for a wonderful future.

Best wishes for an enjoyable luncheon.

Sincerely,

Rudolph W. Giuliani

Rudolph W. Giuliani
Mayor

Publicity poster for Amato: A Love Affair with Opera.

free hour or two in his schedule, he would show up with his soundman and cameraman to film a scene.

Stephen was also interested in the life Sally and I had outside of the Bowery theatre. He would come up to the Bronx, watch us swim in our pool, and join us at our "famous" Columbus diner for breakfast.

While all of this was going on, I went along with the flow, too busy with my own work to pay too much attention to what Stephen was up to. Within two years, the work was completed. One day, he came to show me the finished work (minus many boxes of film that never made it into the final film). It is hard to describe my initial reaction. I was proud of what it showed of our accomplishments, but I was also embarrassed, because I thought it showed me off too much. I did recognize what a fair representation it was, though, since it showed the combination of warmth and hard work it took to make the company what it was.

I shall always be indebted to Stephen Ives for believing in and recording the story of the Amato Opera. *Amato: A Love Affair with Opera* was the winner of the 2001 Audience Award at the Doubletake Film Festival. It was also an official selection of the

2001 Los Angeles Film Festival and the 2001 Side-By-Southwest Film Festival. *Variety* said about the documentary:

> A married couple and partnership has rarely seemed happier or more fulfilling on screen . . .

The result for us was SOLD OUT signs at all performances.

And, yet, there was also a note of sadness to it all, too, since Sally never got to see the documentary that she was so much a part of. People didn't know this at the time, but Sally had been fighting cancer for about 10 years. She fought hard against the disease and kept on working at the theatre all through those years, never losing her sense of humor and her love of all the people who had become her opera family, but her battle came to an end on August 16, 2000.

Photo: Frank Szymanski

Part VIII:

The End of an Era—And Looking Forward!

WITH my dear wife's passing in 2000, I had to make the most difficult decision of my life. I had just reached 80 years of age, with 57 years of involvement in opera, either as a singer, teacher, or impresario. I kept asking myself how much longer I could keep up this schedule.

I have always worried that health issues might someday mean that I would have to stop work at the company. The Amato Opera schedule was a very long and difficult one to sustain. Ever since my operations as a teenager, I have had health problems, so I always worried that these issues could interfere with the smooth running of the company. Luckily, I had trusted assistants, like Ricky and Richard, who helped me feel that there were safe hands I could count on in the case of an emergency, but they both had their own health issues. Some of my conducting assistants, I knew, could take over a rehearsal or a performance if need be and I tried to train some of my singers to stage direct in a pinch. But finding someone who could take over the helm of the company was quite a different matter.

Both Sally and I always hoped that the company would continue with its intimate family atmosphere—always remaining "Small But Oh So Grand!" To both of our regrets, we had no children of our own to pass on our legacy. Because I felt strongly that the company should remain within the family, I turned to my nephew Richard Leighton (son of Sally's sister Margie), who already was established as a singer and stage director, to handle the artistic side of the business, and to my niece Irene Frydel Kim (daughter of Sally's sister Ann) to oversee the box office, office, and daily operations. I invited both to become part of the company's paid staff. Meanwhile, I continued as general manager and artistic director, planning all the opera presentations.

Since he had been a young boy, Richard had performed with the Amato Opera, and I had the opportunity to watch him grow as an artist. Richard got busy quickly, staging and directing a new production of *Faust* and the American premieres of Kalmanoff's *The Empty Bottle* and Donald Grantham's *The Boor*. All three were well-received and highly praised. Bill Zakariasen (*New York Daily News*) mentioned in his review of *The Empty Bottle* that "Richard Leighton's direction for the miniscule stage is a miracle of fluidity, while the sets of Richard Cerullo amaze the eye."

Working with the children's chorus. My nephew Richard Leighton is the second from the left.

The Empty Bottle, directed by Richard Leighton.

But, much to my regret, it soon became clear to me that the new arrangement with Richard and Irene wasn't going to work. After about a year, the friction, criticism, and malcontent existing between the two of them became a considerable problem. It became obvious that they were not going to be able to work as a team to continue the company.

Matters only grew worse. Despite my high esteem for Richard's talent, I could not agree with him over the way he handled young singers. He had very little patience in general, and even less with novices, and he tended to terrorize young people when they made errors, rather than give helpful advice to guide them in achieving the results he wanted. Singers working with Richard who gave generously of their time were becoming affected by the criticism and lack of appreciation of their efforts. Discouragement among the members of the company was beginning to be obvious. This was a tremendous shame, because Richard's great talent was apparent. I tried to give him the benefit of my experience to guide him to work more constructively, but, unfortunately, he only ignored any suggestions I made as general manager and producer.

My attempts to lessen my workload were failing, as I couldn't run the company and control Richard at the same time. It finally came to the point where the board approved my reluctant decision to release him from the company. That being said, I must add that, to this day, I'm convinced that if Richard had been willing to take constructive criticism, adopt some better methods of working with young people, and had been able to control himself better when acting as a teacher and director, he would have been the ideal person—and possibly the only person—to carry on the Amato Opera.

While all of this had been going on, Irene's parents had been in failing health, and when Irene's husband, John Kim, lost his teaching job in Vermont, I invited them all to stay at my house in City Island. Now, with Richard's departure, Irene, in addition to her regular duties, was left in control of the business and financial operations of the company and added the functions of taking charge of costumes and the Operas-in-Brief.

At this point, my original plan was altered to have Irene enlarge her opera repertoire and improve her Italian and French diction. The most important thing for me, though, was that Irene arrange her work schedule so that she could audit, by sitting in the first row of the theatre for the evening cast rehearsals—observing and learning the ins and outs of putting on an opera. This way, I would be able to guide her on the spot, give her notes and tips, try to interpret for her what was going on, and teach her what she needed to know during the rehearsal process itself. I felt this was absolutely necessary if she were to learn even some small part of the skills necessary to assume a leadership role in the company.

After a few weeks of attendance, Irene stopped coming to rehearsals. She claimed that she could watch upstairs on closed-circuit television in the office while doing her other chores. I strongly disagreed and pleaded with her, then insisted that she follow my express wish that she keep attending, but she was not willing to do so.

During the next few years, Irene directed one annual presentation of Menotti's *Amahl and the Night Visitors* and, whenever her physical condition permitted, also narrated Opera-in-Brief presentations. In June of 2005, Irene directed and produced Zeke Hecker's children's opera, *The Forest*, which required 12 children performers and four adults in solo and ensemble numbers. I saw this venture as a much-needed beginning of a permanent children's opera theatre. I gave Irene a great deal of encouragement to continue this project, but this too was all in vain. She soon lost interest and the children's theatre was forgotten.

This part of the story is not easy or pleasant for me to tell. I was getting older and my worries about my health and my ability to continue leading the company kept increasing. I desperately wanted the arrangement with Irene to work out.

I was paying both Irene and her husband a regular salary to help with the company; I gave them the use of a van to facilitate their trips to and from the theatre; and they continued to live rent-free in my home. But my worries only mounted. What if I became incapacitated in the middle of a season and Irene had to carry on without me for periods of time? In case I was not well enough to authorize necessary payments myself, I decided to make sure that her signature would be recognized by the brokerage firm controlling my personal account with all the money Sally and I had been able to save during our long years of work. I also formed an irrevocable trust in Irene's name that would allow the King Avenue home to be held for Irene upon my death, if I did not sell it beforehand; if I did sell the property, then the net proceeds of the sale would go to her after my demise.

Meanwhile, my disillusionment continued to grow. The more I began to think about retiring, the more Irene claimed mounting health problems. Soon she was spending very little time at the theatre. Though she claimed she could do her duties from her bed on King Avenue, where she spent most of her time in front of a television and a computer, it was clear to me that this arrangement was not working. The less Irene worked efficiently or with any interest in the survival of the company, the more I had to ask myself: Can the company support a payroll large enough to sustain the staff that will be necessary for the Amato Opera to continue?

I had to be honest with myself, even if it was painful for me to do so. It seemed to me that Irene and her husband completely lost interest in the company once the irrevocable trust went into effect. Normal, everyday affairs were falling into disarray. For example, longtime patrons were angry at the inefficiencies of the box office and errors with their subscriptions; singers sent in money for videotapes of their performances and never received what they had paid for—or the hurriedly-made tapes were unplayable. I couldn't count on Irene to help with anything I needed. More and more, she claimed her illnesses made it impossible for her to come to the theatre. Financial accounting was becoming slipshod, and I could not get answers about expenditures being authorized from her bed by Irene. In addition, it soon became very apparent that the artistic and musical standards that I had worked long to achieve at the Amato Opera were not being met and would only continue to go downhill under the present arrangement.

As a result, once again, my own theatre responsibilities kept mounting instead of decreasing. I had to recognize that what I had envisioned for the company was not going to take place. With enormous regret, I made the difficult decision to sell the building at 319 Bowery, and, in March of 2009, I terminated Irene and John Kim's employment at the theatre and the Amato Opera board voted to remove them from their positions as officers and members of the Board of Directors. I had to accept, much as I didn't want to do so, that the Amato Opera was going to close its doors at the end of the 2009 season.

All this time, Irene, her husband, and her father (her mother had passed away by this time) continued to live in my house. At this point, I asked them to leave so I could begin a peaceful retirement, but they refused. I had to take legal counsel and commence eviction proceedings against them—a long and difficult process that consumed a great deal of time and money, and was, in addition, physically draining and emotionally debilitating.

Irene countered by refusing to allow me access to my personal investment account. I had not realized that, by adding her signature, it meant that she would have to approve any transactions going forward. We ended up, as required by law, submitting to arbitration and, I believe, to keep the peace, the arbitrator awarded Irene half of the money Sally and I had scrimped and saved throughout our lifetimes, even though she had never contributed a single penny to the total. I'm glad Sally never lived to see what took place.

***

All this being said, the last decade of the Bowery theatre still brought me a great many pleasurable experiences. As is often the case with me, this makes me think of so many people who played a significant part in the later years of the company.

As we were looking toward our 2004-2005 season, I found myself without a costume director when longtime associate Renata Podolec left the company for a well-paying job at Broadway houses— and a husband. Taking advantage of the electronic age, my friend Frank Szymanski suggested that we put a request for a costume designer on the internet. Rineke Akkerhuis, originally from the Netherlands, was living just a few short blocks away from the theatre (a great asset for us), and she gave us a call. As she reminds me, her first attempt to meet was somewhat discouraging, since she was told to call back in two weeks, because we didn't have any stairs at the time (we were in the process of replacing our staircase). But she was brave, called again, and came in one day to look us over, even though she knew that there wasn't much money involved. We immediately hit it off and she agreed to join us. Right away, she got busy designing and executing costumes for *The Magic Flute*, and then about 25 children's costumes for *The Forest*. From then on, Rineke stayed with us.

I was very happy to have Rineke working with us, as she carried on the high artistic standards that Sally had brought to the costume department. She understood right away that the size of the Bowery theatre meant that the audience was very close and could see things like a frayed hem or an exposed zipper—details that might not be seen in a big house. In addition, a bright part of my day was having brunch with her, when we would plan and solve whatever problems we saw coming up. Rineke, in her generous way,

Two of Rineke Akkerhuis' costumes for Cosi fan tutte.

Rineke Akkerhuis was always asked by singers to take their pictures. Here she got an interesting "art" shot as she captured herself in the mirror snapping a photo.

would bring me little tidbits, like the special bread she knew I liked, or some treats she would cook up for us. This brunch ritual is one we still continue to enjoy when time and distance allow.

Ross Solomon in Merry Widow.

Photo: Harald Schrader

A big headache for an opera impresario is when an indisposed singer cancels at short notice. This happens quite often—especially with tenors. Because of the unnaturally high range, tenors are always particularly worried about vocal production. That's not so good for an opera company, where the show must go on, despite a lead singer's misgivings. Starting with the 1998-99 season, the Amato Opera was most fortunate to have Ross Solomon on its roster—a leading tenor with a repertoire of both the lyric-spinto and dramatic roles who is also (in keeping with his love of baseball) a great pinch hitter. Since his debut as Radames in *Aida,* Ross many times put aside the responsibilities of his upstate New York law practice when a tenor emergency arose,

Ross Solomon as Canio in I Pagliacci.

got into his car and drove for two hours to the theatre, put on make-up and his costume, *molto spirito*, and was ready for the curtain to go up. It has been the reliability of this type of artist, with their respect and love for the Amato Opera, that prevented us from cancelling performances. Possessing the combination of excellent musicianship and a strong, exciting, secure, high tenor voice with a vocal technique allowing him to sing a wide range of roles, Ross saved the day for us many a time—and the resulting pre-performance frenzy backstage always translated itself into great, exciting opera onstage! Ross has also become a dear friend as well as a legal advisor to the Amato Opera and the Sally Amato Opera Guild.

Another tenor who could always be counted on was Mark Franko-Filipasic. All my prima donnas loved singing with him, because he was such a sensitive and musical colleague. Mark first came to the company for our 1991 *Carmen*, and he was a regular member of the company from then on. I loved the way Mark prepared himself. Even though he had a demanding job, Mark was always in the house two to three hours before showtime. He would dress and get made up early and then go up to the top floor of the theatre so he could vocalise without disturbing anyone else.

Mark Franko-Filipasic in Act I of La Boheme.

Photo: David Wentworth

Since I am telling tenor stories, I must go back some years to mention Wesley Swails, who started his career with us and then went on to Europe, singing at La Scala. He was a great Canio—and managed one night to handle what could have been an embarrassing occurrence at Amato Opera. In the middle of his great Act II aria, he took a particularly deep breath and his pants fell down right to the ground, exposing his red polka-dot drawers. The audience began snickering. Wesley simply stepped out of his pants and finished the remainder of the act in his shorts. He was rewarded with a standing ovation.

Wesley has become the source of one of those recurring lines that always brings a chuckle to my family and close friends. One night, Sally and I were in Rome, attending the open-air theatre. Still suffering from jet lag, I couldn't manage to keep awake for the whole performance, so we left early, intending to head back to the hotel for a good night's sleep.

As I walked out of the theatre, I heard my name being shouted out loudly, in tones that could not be mistaken for anything other than a tenor voice. There was Wesley, who insisted that we go to a cafe to talk. My eyelids were drooping and I could think of nothing more attractive than bed, but Wesley insisted. For hours and hours, he regaled us with stories of his European successes—always prefaced by the line, "In all modesty. . . ." Forever after, all in fun, of course, my family would preface tales of personal successes with that line: "In all modesty. . . ."

The last decade of the Amato Opera also brought Andrew Whitfield to the conducting staff of the company. He originally came to join the vocal ensemble on the recommendation of his friend, Joseph Marchese, who served as my assistant conductor for a number of years. When it was time for Joe to move on, though he continued to come back as a guest conductor for many of our performances, he suggested that Andrew take over his responsibilities, feeling that his friend had a talent for conducting.

Like Joe, Andrew had a good conducting technique. In addition, Andrew never intended to learn the staging of an opera as a whole, but he was so brilliant that he picked it up almost without trying. He proved this one night when he had to step into the bass role of the Marquis in *La Forza del Destino*. The Marquis has more than once proven to be a problem, since he is the first one to sing in the opera, and, in our production, he needs to be in place as soon as the Overture begins. (Once, I had to sing the role myself from the pit when the bass didn't show up in time.) On this particular night, the singer playing the Marquis wasn't in the house when the curtain was about to go up. Andrew, who sang lyric tenor roles for me, was

Andrew Whitfield (l.) and Garth Taylor (r.) in Die Fledermaus.

quickly thrown into a costume and a wig while the overture was playing, we tossed him out on stage, and he sang the bass role of the Marquis from memory—and did all the staging and music perfectly!

If that weren't enough, Andrew's degree from Boston College was originally for violin. Many nights, he played the violin solo for us in *The Merry Widow*. He would stop conducting and I would hand him the violin. When he was finished, he stepped back into the pit and continued conducting!

A funny story that involved Andrew and his pal Joseph Marchese took place one day when Andrew was playing the role of Dr. Blind in *Die Fledermaus*. When his entrance came, he was nowhere to be found. Luckily, the opera is a comedy. With the audience listening in, I started announcing loudly over the intercom: "Calling Dr. Blind! Calling Dr. Blind" Where was Andrew?—upstairs on the second floor, deep in a discussion about conducting Wagner with Joe Marchese. As quickly as he could, Andrew ran down the stairs and threw himself on stage. He began singing, improvising the lyric, "Our elevator is out of order!" The audience burst into laughter and applause. Of course, we only *wished* we had an elevator at 319 Bowery!

This is a good time for me to introduce Rochelle Mancini, who has been working with me on this memoir, where she has been able to use her expertise as a writer and editor to help me tell my story—a feat I could never have accomplished without her. That wasn't how I first met Rochelle, though. She originally came to the company in 2000, when I cast her as Leonora in *Il Trovatore*, and she sang regularly with us from then on in the more dramatic soprano repertoire.

Perhaps my favorite role Rochelle sang for me was another Leonora, this time the heroine in *La Forza del Destino*. As usual, this brings up a story. It was always very difficult for me to get sopranos to understand certain interpretive moments in *Forza*. In keeping with the title of the opera, destiny is rather a cruel taskmaster in this work. Nothing goes well for the heroine, who starts out in anguish over deceiving her father, becomes a hermit, and finally gets stabbed to death by her brother at the very moment when she finally meets up once again with the lover she thought was dead, after being separated for years (even though it turns out he has become a monk and has been close by all the time). Hard fate, indeed!

Rochelle Mancini as Leonora in La Forza del Destino.

There is a line in the famous last-act aria, "Pace, pace," in which Leonora comments about the meager bread that is left for her each week at her hermit's retreat: *"Misero pane, a prolungarmi vieni la sconsolata vita"* ("wretched bread, you come to prolong my miserable life"). It always bothered me that, even on recordings by top artists, this line tends to be shouted out angrily. I even had a talented young soprano who, at her audition, actually kicked the bread across the stage at that point. I didn't have to explain these kinds of niceties to Rochelle, whose dramatic instincts led her to understand that the line was almost an aside—a commentary on the quiet misery of this heroine's life.

Our 2005 *Forza* was the first production to use supertitles. Earlier on, I had been adamant about not installing a supertitle system, because I was concerned that if audiences were looking up and down to read about what was happening instead of focusing on what was taking place onstage, it would distract from the music and the action. But my audiences kept asking for it. The cost of a

commercial supertitle system like the one used at the Met, was pro-
hibitive, but, once again, a tenor saved the day. Nick Incarnato, a
dramatic tenor who is over six feet tall (not so common among tenors) also happens to be a sound engineer. He came up with a system
that served us well. And, I have to admit, supertitles attracted new
young people to the theatre.

The last decade at the Bowery theatre also brought a brand
new production, *Elisir d'Amore*, which I had never produced before.
It was a fun production that allowed me to showcase the talents of
some of our new artists. I particularly enjoyed that I was able to use
my Italian birthplace, the town of Minori, as a model in painting the
set for the show. Just as I remembered it, I put Ravello up on the
mountaintop in the backdrop, and made sure to paint in my house
and my beloved lemon trees. Whenever we did the opera, I found
myself thinking of child-
hood memories.

*Trudy Wodinsky (left) and Alan Gordon
Smulen (center) in* Elisir d'Amore.

The *Elisir* photo shown
here makes me think espe-
cially of Trudy Wodinsky,
who sang coloratura and
lyric roles for many years for
us. She has a gift for comic
roles, is a great musician,
and she could always make
the audience respond to her
exuberance onstage.

I must also mention an-
other leading lady, Alicia
Alexander, who joined us in
1988. She first sang Nanetta

in *Falstaff* and went on to sing some of our most memorable performances of Violetta, Mimi, and Gilda. In addition to all the high praise from the critics, I add my own high praise for all her cooperation and the many hours she gave of her time working in the box office.

Photo: Konstantin Moskalenko

Those last years were busy ones for me, and they also resulted in some memorable performances of old standards, including, among many others,

Alicia Alexander (l.) as Alice Ford in the Falstaff *letter scene, with Ann Boney (Mistress Quickly)(r.).*

Marriage of Figaro, Don Giovanni, Il Trovatore, Aida, Tosca, Carmen, and *La Bohème.* Also very popular with our audiences in those years were our holiday *Die Fledermaus* and *Merry Widow* performances.

Doing the standard repertoire in those years always gave me

an opportunity to think back on countless other stagings we had done of the same shows over the years and some of the funny things that had occurred, even though they didn't always seem so funny when they were actually happening.

One priceless story that went down in Amato Opera mythology had to do with the crucial entrance of the Commendatore in the Epilogue of *Don Giovanni.* What

I loved clowning around as Alfred in Die Fledermaus.

An old photo of the crucial entrance of the Commendatore in the Epilogue of Don Giovanni.

could be more serious than the statue of the man the Don had killed in the first act coming back to claim the hero's wretched soul in the last act, dragging him down through the trapdoor to the fiery pits of hell? Well, one night, the terrifying effect didn't come off the way it was supposed to because of a mechanical error. The way it worked was this: in pitch darkness backstage, while the ensemble was singing the Finale, the Commendatore, all dressed up menacingly as a statue in armor and a visor, had to get on the horse and the two were drawn onto the stage. The bass did exactly what he was supposed to do, but, on this particular night, the horse hadn't been preset properly. That meant that at the final tableau of the opera, the first thing the audience saw was the rear of the horse, with the extremely grandiose Commendatore seated facing his horse's tail!

Another mishap involving *Don Giovanni* also took place at the end of the opera. The Finale called for many gimmicks and much stage business, including quite a number of electrical effects, especially at the climax, when the Don, accompanied by screams, disappeared into "hell" via the trapdoor, while the ceiling fell and a complete blackout took place onstage.

As I had staged it, once the Epilogue picks up, all the lights begin to come back on. One night that didn't happen as planned. The technician had forgotten to turn off the main switches that were, as a result, drawing much too much power during the big effect. What hap-

pened was that, after a good minute of overload, we got an unplanned *second* blackout, leaving no lights on the music stands in the orchestra pit. Luckily, it wasn't open-

Masetto (center, Peter De Simone) and his cronies seeking Don Giovanni in the dark. Ricky Figueroa is second from the left.

Photo: David Wentworth

ing night, but about the 10th performance in the series of 12 shows. My wonderful orchestra just continued to play by memory in the pitch darkness of the pit. As for me, I had to run back to the main switches, make the necessary corrections, then find my way back into the pit and catch up with my orchestra, which was still playing as if nothing at all had happened!

Then, of course, there was the memorable *Madama Butterfly* when our child (whose name is appropriately 'Trouble') didn't show up on time. Usually, I covered myself by having plenty of substitutes in the house, but young children are particularly unpredictable and that day there was no extra child ready to go on as Butterfly's son. What could we do? Well, they don't say that necessity is the mother of invention for nothing. In anticipation (as was my habit), I had a big photo of a child waiting on the prop table, ready to be handed to the poor Butterfly. When the child showed up later in the course of the show, he stepped in at an appropriate time. The really strange thing was that the audience didn't seem to mind in the slightest!

And how can I resist telling about a famous Amato Opera mishap that took place in *Faust*. The staging in the very first scene called for an "explosion" in the left stage balcony on Mephistophélès' entrance. On one memorable day, we had more than we bargained for when the electrical powder box that created the smoke for the explosion managed, in the process, to ignite a piece of styrofoam that shouldn't have been there in the first place. The alarmed audience was perfectly aware that a fire had broken out, but neither Faust (Vincent Titone) nor Mephistophélès (Konstantin Moskalenko) had a clue what was happening. They just continued to sing, wondering what the fuss was all about. While the music played on, I had to jump up on stage and climb the ladder to the stage balcony and put out the fire with my bare hands—and, believe me, it was hot! Then, as casually as possible, I headed back into the pit and continued conducting as if nothing special had happened.

When you start telling one story, you have to tell another: How about the time the orchestra was playing the dramatic phrases that give the feeling that Radames is on horseback, racing to meet his beloved at his entrance in the Act III Nile Scene of *Aida*? Well, one night, because of the close quarters backstage, a wire that held the set in place caught in the tenor's costume. No sooner had he made this vital entrance than, like a spring—*sproing!*—he was pulled offstage by the wire, singing all the while. Only once the wire was untangled was he able to re-enter, completing his *molto* dramatic entrance.

Then there was a performance of *Tosca* that set a record of two major mishaps for the same singer in the same scene. Both involved the baritone playing Baron Scarpia, who was on leave from his regular job as a member of the Metropolitan Opera ensemble. At the climactic point in the second act of *Tosca*, when Scarpia fell to the floor after being stabbed by Tosca, and at a mo-

Sabrina Palladino as Tosca, Act II.

ment that is definitely not supposed to be funny, his wig fell right off his head. As if that weren't enough, he had decided, without my knowledge, to use his own version of the stage blood that was preset in his shirt, ready to look very real when Floria Tosca's knife delivered his deathblow. But, instead of using our customary set-up, he decided to use catsup, which splashed out all over the set. Since we had a good ventilation system, it meant that everyone in the audience could share in the beautiful odor that spread through the theatre, making Scarpia smell like a hamburger ready to be eaten.

Believe me, I spent many, many hours trying to anticipate things that could go wrong in a performance. One thing I always did for *Tosca* performances was have two separate people set up backstage for the execution scene gun cue—one regular and one backup. In addition, we had someone ready with a huge hammer and a sounding board so that, simultaneously, on cue, all three would make a powerful noise. That way, I knew there would be a sufficient sound of a gunshot. I started this system years before when, in a Don Carlo at the Metropolitan Opera, the shot never went off when Rodrigo was supposed to be killed. Ever since that time, I made sure to have three fallbacks!

I also kept another trick on hand for the *Tosca* execution scene. We put a firecracker in the barrel of each "rifle," which we connected backstage to an electric line once everybody was in place. This created quite an effect, for as all the firecrackers went off on cue, sparklers also came from the barrels of the guns.

And yet, for all the planning, something always can go wrong—and probably will! I remember the time Konstantin Moskalenko sang his first *Falstaff* for us. We had carefully worked out the section of the action where Sir John hides in the laundry basket before being dumped into the Thames, and I had the basket preset exactly right at the curtain line, camouflaged by the main curtain. The timing was crucial. Falstaff would duck into the basket and was supposed to sneak out through a movable panel behind the curtain and hide backstage in time for the servants to pick up the basket and go through the motions of dumping it out into the river. Even though we had rehearsed it carefully, during the performance, Konstantin could be clearly seen sneaking up the side steps of the stage, in full view of the audience, before disappearing into the wings. It completely ruined the illusion of Sir John being dumped ignominiously into the river. I was so disgusted I never got around to asking him what was going on in his head when he either nervously, innocently, or intentionally decided to alter the staging.

Since the last show we did at the Bowery theatre was *The Marriage of Figaro*, I must take one more opportunity to mention mishaps that took place in that opera. During one Act II Finale many years ago, we put on quite a show. Our Figaro was a strapping 6-foot, 8-inch bass-baritone. The staging calls for him, in his anger, to throw Bartolo's legal papers up into the air. That day, he was so enthusiastic that, in so doing, he dislocated his shoulder and we had to rush him to the hospital. Now *The Marriage of Figaro* is a very long opera. The only thing we could do was for me—a 5-foot, 3-inch tenor—to step into his role. Needless to say, this was quite difficult for the audience to swallow. Luckily, they were very appreciative. This wasn't the end of the mental imagination that had to take place in that performance though, because, by the time we reached Act IV, the original Figaro was back from the hospital in time to finish the opera—in a sling!

A final story is about the very last performance we gave at the Bowery theatre. It also allows me to give a little "dissertation" about a particularly beloved moment in opera, and it has to do with the value of a corona.

Photo: Corinta Koltula

Saying goodnight to the audience at the end of our last New Year's gala, 2009.

A corona is a musical silent pause, and it can be a most expressive musical tool. When a corona is set over a note, it has been my practice to hold that note a little less than twice its original value—always keeping good taste in mind. To judge and interpret the corona in a silent moment, the conductor needs to have a good theatrical understanding of the play and the characters within it.

The most unobserved corona, I believe, is the one in the Finale of the *Marriage of Figaro*, on the closing phrases of the last exchange between the Count and the Countess. The great Count is on his knees, for the first time truly understanding the nobility of his wife. He begs her to forgive him for his escapades and his lack of trust, despite her constant faithfulness. Humbly, he reaches out to the Countess, beseeching her to take his outstretched hand in forgiveness.

The Count must swallow all his embarrassment and unhappiness to address his wife, in full view of his court, which stands watching in silence. At this climactic point in the score, there is a corona, completely stopping all the music and action for a moment. This pause, for me, is one of the greatest and most expressive in all of opera. I staged it so that, with a deep silence that must last at least 4-5 seconds, the Countess slowly extends her hand to her husband's outstretched, supplicating hand as she delivers her line, in the Ruth and Thomas Martin English translation we always used: "How could I refuse it, my heart speaks for you." All of the constant movement and scheming of the opera is resolved in this instant of peace and serenity. It is a moment in the opera that I always loved so much as an artist and waited for with great anticipation at each performance. Thank you, Mozart!

In our crucial final performance of the Amato Opera, all my careful rehearsal preparation went for nought as the overly-eager soprano neglected to observe this corona. In my frustration, I was heard quite loudly to whisper, "Oh my God—no!"

The stories could go on and on—and, for me, they do—but all things must eventually come to an end. Much as it was hard for me to imagine that the days of striking sets and setting up new shows were finally over, I found myself closing the gold stage curtain for the last time after the matinée on May 31, 2009. Present and past cast members joined hands on stage, tears were shed, and I looked out at a packed house, only to see row after row of audience members who had been coming to Amato Opera performances for years and years—all standing, cheering, and with tears in their eyes. We all knew that it was the end of an era.

As for me, I add a personal note. As I left the theatre that evening, I recalled Sally's voice telling me something she always used to repeat when I stayed awake too late at night thinking about a score—which was most of the time. It seemed an appropriate thought

Last curtain call at the Bowery theatre.
(l. to r.) Trudy Wodinsky, Mark Freiman (and a little Freiman), me, Helen Van Time, and Mark Bentley.

at this moment. "Put the lights out now, Tony," she would say. "You have been in bed now too long with Carmen or Manon."

***

While it was a relief to give up my grueling theatre schedule, I found I really had no desire to cease working in the field I loved so much. I found it hard to stop being interested in helping young singers. To carry through on dreams Sally and I had long discussed, I began to think of holding a few competitions a year, using the Amato Opera funds to provide scholarships for young artists. Maybe also in my mind was the desire to keep the Amato Opera name alive in the music circles. My main thought was not the prize amounts, though, since whatever we could provide would still be small when it comes to the cost of providing the training that young performers need.

In 2010, we held the first Sally and Anthony Amato Opera Scholarship Competiton for singers. I was extremely pleased by the quality of the young people who applied. They were so good that it was very difficult to choose the finalists. The answer I came up with was to create more prizes and award larger amounts of money to the deserving winners. I was very proud that all of our five finalists, along with four of the semi-finalists, received cash awards so badly needed by all young singers. We ended up giving out $24,000 in prize money.

The finalists performed at a gala luncheon for our guest judges: George Shirley, Mignon Dunn, and Eve Queler. What fine choices they were as judges! The conductor Eve Queler has brought such wonderful lesser-known music and exciting new voices to New York City. As for George Shirley and Mignon Dunn, they both sang for the Amato Opera early in their careers, and never forgot us, even when they achieved so much success later on. I would like to

The 2010 Sally and Anthony Amato Opera Scholarship Competition gala.
(l. to r.) me, my brother Albert's wife Zallee, Albert, and George Shirley.

point out that George Shirley, possessor of a great voice and a great friend, flew into town from the Midwest on a one-day round trip, just to be with us for the competition. It was a great honor to have three such wonderful and esteemed judges.

The large amount of money it requires to keep presenting such competitions gradually made me change my thoughts and I began to wonder: Why not set up a course with a reputable school to try to keep alive my system of putting an opera together? Not wishing to see the funds of the Amato Opera diminish as greatly as they do in providing major cash awards, I thought this might be a better way to leave a legacy for the future and to reach more people. I am pleased to say that Manhattan School of Music was very receptive to the plan, and we have set up a named legacy endowment, called 'The Sally and Anthony Amato Program Fund: Preparing for the Opera World.' This fund will establish a program for young singers, pianists, and conductors, where they will be trained in my system in order to perform Operas-in-Brief at the school and through Manhattan School of Music's outreach program at elementary and secondary schools in New York City. It makes me feel very good to know that this program will continue long into the future, even when I no longer can or wish to lead it myself.

As for now, since I am only 90 years old as I write this, I look forward to teaching these classes, especially with the staff that will be present to pick up my system and pass it on. It will provide a basic understanding of a role for young artists that they can take anywhere, blending it with any direction that they are given in other productions. To me, this is one of the most important things about the system I have developed. It joins together all the different elements of an opera—singing, directing, conducting—and makes people work together to realize the responsibilities of all the others who are part of the production. Pianists must know what the singers are doing; the stage director and conductor work together under one supervisor; and, only by joining together, do all come to understand not only their own contribution, but grasp the language and jobs of the others. I truly believe that only by such a unified system of working together can a fine production be achieved.

I am pleased that the Amato Opera board agreed with me about the direction for the future, and they voted to turn over the remaining funds in the company to the Manhattan School of Music named legacy endowment. I am also much encouraged by the reaction of the Manhattan School of Music officers. We have already chosen *The Magic Flute* as our first opera—and I can't wait to get started in January 2011. All in all, this isn't a bad way to go into retirement!

Part IX:

Why It All Worked

A
S I look back, I can't help thinking about how the Amato Opera managed to thrive over a period of 61 years, when so many other small opera companies disappeared from New York City's cultural world.

One thing I know is that, through the difficult early years and during times of financial setbacks, it worked because Sally was at my side. Because the company was both our lifework and our joy, we were able to devote all of our time and effort to building on our aspirations. The company was our work and our play—our every day and our special days. I was immeasurably blessed to have a partner in Sally who could share my dreams and yet still call me completely crazy when those dreams occasionally (oh, maybe a little more than occasionally) threatened to get out of hand.

Perhaps Sally sometimes wished (as she expressed in Stephen Ives' documentary *Amato: A Love Affair with Opera*) that I could have had a bigger theatre, orchestra, and audience than what would fit into the Smallest Grand Opera in the World. But, if I look at my life realistically and put aside The-Sky-Is-The-Limit aspirations that all young artists tend to have, I realize that we created a model that worked for us at the Bowery theatre. When I had tried to go bigger, early in my career, the financial headaches were also bigger, the crises that came with working with stars in the field not to my liking, and the need to please so many others with a financial stake in each project's success so much more difficult and time-consuming. Each "big time" obstacle only meant the less time available to produce opera the way I wanted to do it, and the less it was possible to maintain my own personal standards of excellence.

Our success was due to a combination of hard work and business savvy. Because starting a company means a sacrifice of personal savings and a leap into the unknown, it takes a special kind of moxy, and maybe the end of World War II brought that out in a lot of us postwar "entrepreneurs." Running an opera company is no place for a separate day job to support one's after-work aspirations. Sally and I just plunged in. We both were used to making do with little, and we thought it was worth giving the attempt our all. Whether that was smart or not is another question, but, in our case, it worked. Another factor was something that perhaps had more to do with my own background, even before I was a teenager, helping my father feed his family at the diner, or to my life as a butcher at 16, reusing paper bags to cut down on costs. It gave me a business sense that always forced me to balance artistic desires with cold, hard necessity.

And so, "Small But Oh So Grand" was our mantra—along with "Always Anticipate!" This is what kept me in balance, never allowing artistic vanity to get the better of what we could reasonably accomplish—even though we made sure we could sometimes indulge ourselves in an exciting new project. Even then, I always counted in the benefits of getting new reviews and PR (increased ticket sales, increased audience demand, attracting new artists who wanted the opportunity to be involved in more exotic repertoire) when I contemplated satisfying my own desires to take on a new production.

Our system was refined over the years until we had a reliable method of filling the theatre. It started with careful planning of the upcoming year's performance schedule. The season-opening opera was usually a popular one with strong box office appeal. This was aimed at attracting our patrons back after the two-month summer break, and getting them used to their routine of regularly coming to see our operas again. Usually, the choice of the opening opera would be one requiring lyric singers (of which we had an abundance) and a small chorus. My chorus members would be returning from summer vacation in dribs and drabs, so I had to play it safe with operas that didn't require huge choruses.

The second opera on the schedule would be a heavier one, keeping our dramatic singers busy, and allowing enough time to prepare the weightier chorus music. This would take us to mid-December.

During the holiday season, the choice was always a fun and happy opera, such as *Barber, Fledermaus*, or *Merry Widow*. The exception was an occasional *La Boheme*, the most performed opera in our repertoire and a favorite of audiences over the years no matter when we scheduled it. For New Year's Eve, we would have a gala that brought in additional money, even though coordinating the opera with wining and dining our paying guests was not an easy matter.

The short mid-January to mid-February recess was always the ideal time to make plans for adding a new production to the repertoire—often an American premiere or a revival—which required more preparation and more rehearsals for the singers and production staff. Because this opera was often a novelty, we could count on more press coverage for these productions.

The fifth and sixth operas for the season were always from the standard repertoire, alternating an opera for the lyric singers with another for more dramatic singers.

During the season, I tried to present well-rounded repertoire, but usually Verdi, Puccini, and Mozart operas won out. Still, I often included a Donizetti opera, and *Carmen* and *Barber of Seville* were

*Richard Cerullo's painting of Verdi,
patron saint of the Amato Opera.*

regulars over the years. If you have noticed that there wasn't much time off, you would be right. Our breaks in January and over the summer were spent either preparing a big new project or juggling all the many people we would be casting for the upcoming season.

And if it sounds like we put on a lot of performances (counting Operas-in-Brief, it amounted to close to 100 shows a year, and sometimes more), that is, in fact, correct. With a seating capacity of only 107 seats at the Bowery theatre, our commitment to keeping the admission price low, and the mounting expenses of the building and productions, even with full houses there was just so much income that could be taken in at the box office. If the performance was not 90-95 percent sold, we were in trouble. Stipends for the cast, including solo singers, 30 chorus members, an orchestra of 10, and a stage and box office staff of 10 people kept mounting up to quite a figure—$700 to $800 per performance. Added to that were building taxes, utilities, maintenance, and insurance.

We were able to obtain some additional income from the raffle drawing we would hold at intermission, which people always enjoyed. I liked to have members of the children's chorus draw the prizes from one of our fancy stage hats. We always had a good time during the raffle, which provided lots of laughs for our audience. The prizes would be Amato Opera tee-shirts, caps, tote bags, and aprons. Even the most elegantly-dressed people in our audiences wouldn't turn down the opportunity to sport one of our tee-shirts!

Of course, it helped a lot during our early years at the Bowery that, by presenting so many different casts, we continuously brought in new public. Singers could be counted on to bring in their friends and family to see them perform. In the early years, this certainly helped us to stay out of the red!

The Amato Opera has always been proud that it never cancelled a single opera in its 61 years of existence (except for one huge snow storm—and we made up that performance at a later date). With so many capable young artists actively seeking a platform in a full-staged opera production before a live audience, we always had the luxury of back-up casting: each opera ran for 12 performances over a period of one month. Of course, this necessitated many live rehearsals, but it also provided covers for indisposed singers; or, as it often happened, if the scheduled artist would have the opportunity to be engaged with a well-paying singing job elsewhere. When that happened, I always released them from their commitment, as long as they answered the following questions: Is this job going to advance your career? If it is not going to do that, then is the financial incentive enough to justify giving up the performance with us? If the answer to either one was "yes," then I advised them to take the job.

In casting the singers, chorus, musicians, and conductors for the run of each 12-show series per opera, our veteran singers would always perform the first six shows of that series, giving the new casts the opportunity to audit many rehearsals and performances before their own dress rehearsal and performance toward the end of the run. This system worked as well for the orchestra, pianists, stage directors, and my assistant conductors.

Much as I wanted to present operas like *Tales of Hoffmann, Andrea Chenier, Aida,* and *La Forza del Destino,* I always had to reassure myself first that I had the artists I needed on the roster to perform these intricate operas. When casting, the primary duty was always to attain a high vocal standard and a well-balanced cast at every performance. In such an intimate theatre as ours, the way the lead singers looked needed to be believable for the novice as well as the more knowledgeable opera public. However, if at times that was impossible to achieve, I learned that the power of an exceptional voice makes the music and voice take over, and the audience becomes oblivious to such issues as people's height or weight.

Casting wasn't always easy. I imagine the name itself, 'Amato' (he who is loved) provided the attraction of many love affairs and marriages—and yes, a few divorces. Since some of my veteran singers stayed with the company for many years, that could present certain problems in casting well-balanced opera performances, since I had to take into consideration not only visual and vocal qualifications, but also social relations when trying to keep all my cast members happy and trouble free. This always made me feel like Figaro in the *Barber of Seville*: "Tony the factotum of the Amato Opera."

Another major factor that I think was important in our success was how much I loved to teach. It was a great joy (if, indeed, it could occasionally be a trial and an aggravation) to try to guide young artists and help them grow. I've seen a number of people fail over the years because they only saw themselves on top as impresarios, and neglected the groundwork necessary to guide and teach young people.

I believe my forte as an opera director was when I got on stage, demonstrating the stage direction and singing the musical phrase. That, for me, was a much better solution, I found, than using a lot of narrative or technical words. It took many years of teaching for me not to keep on insisting on getting the directions exactly right from a young singer at the first or second run-through of a scene. I found that if I gave young artists a few days to digest it all, at their next rehearsal I always saw great results. Many times, I grasped details and little mannerisms in their presentations that I never thought of before, which inspired me as a director so we could go on to the next level of interpretation. That's the mystery of working with grand opera: one never ceases to discover new insight into the masterpieces!

A director must give the artist freedom—along with strong discipline. Many years ago, watching a veteran director work on a scene from *La Traviata*, I became completely frustrated with his directorial approach. He kept insisting that Papa Germont cross to left stage and sit in an exact number of steps! What he should have worked toward was that Germont cross and sit in the mood and meaning of the script and music.

As I've said before, twice a year I would listen to the growing numbers of new singers who would seek to become part of the Amato Opera. This was especially the case as the conservatories turned out more and more artists, but there were fewer and fewer places for them to go to learn their standard repertoire and have the opportunity to perform in full productions with at least a small orchestra.

Many times, inexperienced singers found it difficult to prepare their assigned roles to the level of my approval. My aim was to make them realize that the repertory opera world was very different from how they prepared for an opera in the conservatory. As students, they might have a whole semester to prepare for one production. In the professional opera world, it is a novelty to get more than one stage and musical rehearsal and the director has to know exactly what to do and how to put the show together in a few short hours. The director must be prepared to put across all his ideas to the cast—under pressure sometimes—and often under the restraint of a lack of funds. Young artists must learn quickly how to take in all this information in a short period of time.

The old directors often neglected to give a deeper understanding of the singers' roles and rarely had the opportunity to offer their ideas of the opera, as all that was provided was a piano rehearsal. At performance time, the person drawing the curtain (and often acting as the stage manager) would bark out from the wings: "Enter here—sit there—go there!" etc., and that was it for stage direction.

In order to achieve a cohesive visual opera production, a director must insist from the cast that everybody has the same conception of the story line and one unified style of body movement, which is dictated by the music. When many of the people who worked with me moved on to large opera companies, they realized that our training gave them the groundwork for productions where they weren't given any directions. With the base outline we had worked out, they could apply it to less-than-ideal working situations.

One thing I noticed about young artists was that they usually moved too quickly for the audience to grasp the meaning of what they were doing. For me, the music always dictates the right tempo for the feeling of the movement. Rarely did I think "This is Spain" or "This is France," because the composer had already done that for me.

Because it came naturally to me, I would demonstrate. For example, take Des Grieux's first entrance in *Manon* as he wanders onto the square. I remember having to tell a young tenor who came strutting out onto the stage, "You're walking like a truck driver!" I reminded him that his physical movements had to convey to the audience that his character was about to begin studies for the priesthood. As he turns, he sees for the very first time the young woman—Manon—who will change his life. The music dictates that this scene should be done like a dream sequence, conveying the impression of a young man deep in thought about his future. This was one of the most difficult effects to teach young singers. Most of the time, I found it much easier to go onstage myself and demonstrate how it could be accomplished.

Another thing I used to tell my classes has to do with the expression *"in bocca al lupo"* (literally, "in the mouth to the wolf"), opera's customary "good luck" or "break a leg." Because young singers often unconsciously perform with their eyes either on the floor or on the too-distant ceiling, they shut out the audience from seeing the expression on their faces. So, even though it wasn't my custom to say too much in words to my students, I enjoyed telling them in simple language my own interpretation of *"in bocca al lupo."* I said that the audience represents the wolf, ready to eat you up if you displease them. So, you must project and sing directly to "the wolf," leaving Mr. Lupo with his mouth wide open, exclaiming "Wow! That was great singing and interpretation!" Then I put my final touch on the story for the class: "Don't stand there singing like a *salsiccia* ('sausage' or 'salami')." (In my butcher days, my shop always had sausages and salamis just hanging motionless from the ceiling.)

As described earlier, in order to be ready for rehearsals at our company, there was quite a bit of preparation singers had to do before they were ready to rehearse, learning directions from the master score in addition to simply memorizing their own musical role. Of course, dealing with so many casts for a single production, this kind of background work was absolutely necessary. There was no way I could begin from scratch with a new singer at each successive re-hearsal. But I also hoped this procedure would instill a sense of how much advance preparation a singer needs to put into learning a role. It is definitely not enough just to learn one's lines and music. If you don't have a larger sense of what is happening in an opera, then it will end up being a bunch of people standing around and singing, and it won't come together to create a musical and theatrical whole.

If the individual has the talent and the drive, this system does work. As a point of interest, in the early days of the Amato Opera, it was the custom to assign each new cast four rehearsals before their performance. But here I must quote Dick Deadeye's famous line in *Pinafore*: "It's Human Nature!" With so many rehearsals, I found that the artists never came prepared until the fourth and last rehearsal, so I cut it down first to three, then to two, and finally, to one—and it worked!

I loved instructing the young artists. It was always a great surprise and enjoyment for me to see certain productions of the same opera with young singers working together happily and whole-heartedly as an ensemble, creating an exciting performance that projected over the footlights. With more veteran casts of singers, this rarely happened. More experienced singers are often immersed in their techniques and individual vocal effects, while novices often were open to the feeling of being a part of the creative ensemble process. It is precisely that ensemble process that makes opera good theatre.

This brings me to a favorite topic: the chorus. I've always believed that the chorus is a vital, active participant in the onstage drama of an opera. This may sound strange to people who are used to thinking of an opera chorus as a bunch of people who stand at the edges of the stage, staring at the conductor while singing their lines—and perhaps waving a palm frond or two during *Aida*.

I have always believed that the chorus is a vital, active participant in the onstage drama, and I made it my business to transform my choruses into a throng of real people, who reacted to everything going on around them, moving about naturally and—very importantly—interacting with one another at appropriate times. And, because we had 12 performances at a time of each opera, we had the luxury of making the chorus action evolve over the run. Maybe it was something little, like some physical gesture a chorus member could use to make his particular character come alive during a crowd scene. Sometimes it involved groups of people in a larger movement that would look very powerful to the audience. But, if you think it is difficult to get one tenor or one soprano lead singer to follow a stage direction, just magnify that 30 times when imagining what it took on our small stage to control and maneuver all the chorus members!

I had more trouble with chorus members than with soloists when it came to strange advice from voice teachers. It still annoys me when voice teachers advise students not to sing in a chorus and sometimes even suggest that it is detrimental to the voice. This is a ridiculous idea, and was especially so in our small, intimate theatre, where nobody ever needed to push for volume. Sometimes singers were told that chorus work would hurt them, or divert them from their true calling as lead singers. I found exactly the opposite to be the case. And, although I never tried to teach voice when working with my chorus, I did find myself warning chorus members:

"Sing out—you're crooning and that doesn't make your vocal chords strong" or "Are you saving your voice for Christmas?" That was because they often held back on

Aida *chorus.*

Photo: Harald Schrader

their teachers' advice. For young people, that often puts them more in danger of choking up and really doing damage. The best way I found to get my ideas across, though, was not to talk to young singers about singing or vocal tips, but to sing the phrases myself. People learn best by example.

I will always believe that anyone seeking a career in opera should at some time participate in the chorus in full-staged performances. This provides a true lesson in how many facets there are to learn in the process of becoming a real artist. Maybe there isn't much glamour being on stage as part of a crowd of singers for a young, talented student who is well-advanced vocally and musically. It doesn't help one's ego much. But it is great training and great preparation when the time comes to take on larger roles. Singing in the chorus was how I learned my trade, and I will always be grateful for the invaluable lessons that my chorus experience taught me.

And in talking about the chorus, how can I not include another favorite—the children's chorus. I always felt great joy and satisfaction when working with our children during their chorus rehearsals. At 5 PM, they would rush into the theatre to start rehearsing for the next hour and a half, and when it was over, they would stay for the adults' rehearsal that followed and eagerly watch for hours. It proved to me that all that was needed in order to create a love for opera was

Hansel and Gretel

exposure to it and places like ours where operatic programs were presented.

Another great pleasure for me was in watching children grow up in our company. One standout was Heather Bloch, a pretty little girl who came to the Bowery theatre to dance in *Manon* when she was still very young. Dancing was Heather's primary love and she served the company in many ways over the following years, preparing choreography and dancing solo in our productions. The love for music eventually led her to other aspects of opera and she began to sing in the chorus and take

Heather Bloch in Rigoletto.

on many assisting solo roles. Her original choreography was a great gift to our productions. Her work on choreographing our *La Traviata* and *Tales of Hoffmann* especially stands out in my mind.

Mark Freiman, whose pictures are scattered throughout these pages, was one of the oldest members of the company. He started in our children's chorus and from there went on to the Metropolitan Opera children's chorus, where he sang the Shepherd in *Tosca*. Before his voice changed, I started using him as a super in our productions, so he was able to keep performing until his voice settled into his adult bass-baritone.

Mark Freiman in Lo Schiavo.

Then he moved up to leading roles with us and, from there, into regional theatres all over the country. From his home base in St. Louis, he is now happily married. In an extreme emergency, to replace an indisposed singer, Mark was always ready to jump on a plane and help us out.

Another young person it was fun to watch grow up was Alizon Hull, who came to us right out of college. She remembers her first audition for me, when she sang "Batti, Batti," the Zerlina aria from *Don Giovanni*—hardly the most difficult piece in the soprano repertoire—and proceeded to forget the words not once, but four times! I saw the potential in her, though, and to her amazement, assigned her the role of Micaela in *Carmen*. She was absolutely sure she wouldn't be able to sing the part, but she came to every single rehearsal to watch others in the role, so she would be as prepared as she could be once her turn came for her performance. Still, she was terribly nervous. In rehearsal, she fell through the black curtain of the perch right onto the stage—and burst into tears. "Listen, honey," she tells me I said, "You were nervous, but you knew your stuff!" When a young singer showed the drive to learn and improve, that made all the difference for me.

Photo: Aaron Lee Fineman

(l. to r.) Alizon Hull and Kathy Enders in Falstaff.)

Alizon went on to sing many soprano lead roles with the company over the years. In addition, her father managed a children's theatre, Theatreworks, USA, and he began to produce and distribute our Operas-in-Brief to schools and other locations, including Town Hall. Alizon later married Giovanni Reggioli, who has conducted performances at Washington Opera, Sydney Opera, the Baths of Caracola in Rome, and many other major venues. A secret wish of his was to sing the small (but scene-stealing) part of Antonio in *Marriage of Figaro* in one of our productions, but he was always busy with conducting jobs whenever I might have fulfilled his dream. Still, in his upscale productions, Alizon tells me, he often tells a singer to "try this" when they are at an impasse and, according to Alizon, it is most often what she calls a "Tony direction."

And how can I not be proud of the Sparacio "dynasty." All twelve of them were part of the company, serving as the core for the children's chorus, and growing up with the Amato Opera over the years. As an adult, Cecile played flute with the orchestra through the last season.

Here I am, on the last day at the Bowery theatre, with Mama Sparacio and all twelve of the Sparacio "boys and girls," as I've always called them since they were children.

Over the years, people who worked with the company left New York, the hub of the American art world, and went to other locations in the U.S., sometimes back to their hometowns, where they would open their own small companies and carry on what they had learned. This gave me great satisfaction. It was something I always stressed in my classes. "Learn everything," I always told my students. "Not everyone will make the Metropolitan Opera. Learn all the aspects of the theatre you can, so you can turn to teaching and running other companies. You can't do that just by studying your own role." Not too many paid attention, but some did, and it stood them in good stead. One person, in particular, who got his start at the Amato Opera was a Metropolitan Opera chorus member, Tim Wilson. He later moved into smaller roles at the Met. He eventually retired, along with his wife, who played violin in the Met orchestra. They moved out West, where they opened a school in the Tony Amato tradition. What better joy for a teacher!

***

After many years of observing the problems—and often chaos—that take place in managing large and famous opera organizations, I realize how lucky and privileged I've been acting alone as general manager and director for the intimate Amato Opera. It makes me think of two common sayings: "Too Many Cooks Spoil the Broth," and "The Buck Stops Here."

My own experience has led me to believe that a successful opera company must have one person at its head—the general manager—who makes all business and artistic decisions and oversees every facet of the company. That way, if anything goes wrong, there's only one person to blame. On most important occasions, it is the general manager who must keep all the production directors happy working together toward a successful opera. To do that, he or she must be a politician.

Problematic situations usually begin to arise at the stage rehearsal. Conflicts between the stage director and scenic designer are many: a window or door or a property not where they had been planned; the lighting for each scene; lack of a unified style and period of the opera, etc. All of these issues must be solved and agreed upon in advance. Most importantly, and sometimes overlooked, all directors must coordinate the execution and storage of the sets and other production problems during the performance.

Make-up and wigs are often neglected in a small company, but they were particularly important in our small 107-seat theatre, because all details could be seen closely. The prima donnas are usually the cast members who must be checked most carefully. Using everyday street make-up makes them appear pale under the strong stage lights, yet the wrong or overdone make-up can ruin the illusion. For example, the opera *Carmen* takes place in sunny, warm Seville; *Boheme* must bring to mind a cold Paris winter. It is important to have the correct basic pancake that evokes the proper setting, but that also blends with the skin of the principal and the ensemble members as well.

Maintaining a good wig department is not only an expensive proposition, but it also requires much care and cleaning. In a company like ours, where perhaps three differ-

Wigs ready for a touch-up after a performance.

ent casts could sing the same opera on one weekend, that wasn't an easy task. Say, for example, we needed powdered wigs for *Andrea Chenier*. Three different people might wear the same wig on three successive days. The three probably differ in head size, coloring, and personal preference. Adjustments, as much as possible, would have to be made for each person and the wig prepared for the next wearer.

Directing opera rehearsals, combining the soloists, chorus, stage direction, musical directions, and keeping everybody working calmly and creatively together is an art that, I must admit, took me years of teaching and study and experience interacting with people before I felt composed and prepared enough to do well. Often, the singers would request a different tempo from mine, or would want to hold certain notes a bit longer. My stock answer was always: "Be flexible to whatever the conductor wishes. All conductors differ. Right now, it's good training for you to do it my way." However, through the years, I've learned as a conductor to let young singers express themselves, as long as they retain my musical conception— and, many times, that has led me to blend a new idea into my own, especially when the artist is well-prepared musically and linguistically. This atmosphere of a free exchange of ideas helps to create an exciting performance.

A good stage director must know the script completely— and by that I mean *all* the parts. Having artistic musical instincts is definitely an added asset. I believe the opera director is also greatly benefited by having some kind of a singing voice in addition to acting instincts, in order to demonstrate the emotion of an opera through one's eyes and face in addition to the music.

Another factor that is extremely important in running a small opera company is knowing when it is a wise idea to expand and when to rein in one's ambitions. During our early days, we used two-piano accompaniments for our productions. Even though I would have loved to have an orchestra, I knew that it wasn't a good idea to strain our finances while we were getting started. For quite a while, though, the two-piano arrangement served us well.

As we became more popular, I realized that we needed some instrumental sound from the pit to complete our "Small But Oh So Grand" concept, so, with the help and encouragement of my assistant conductor, Liz Hastings, the Amato Opera Chamber Ensemble was created. Of course, I still had to be very careful and not become *too* grand. This meant many, many hours of preparing a cut-down orchestration to achieve a well-blended sound from the pit. The balance I came up with was one flute and piccolo (doubling), one oboe and English horn (doubling), two clarinets (1st and 2nd), one bassoon, one or two French horns, one trumpet, and, when necessary, one trombone, and—oh yes—always one person at the keyboard, doubling on organ and harpsichord (not to mention providing string sounds).

As the news got around town, more and more young students from New York music schools began to play for us for compensation that finally, in the last years, came to the grand total of $25.00 per show. Again, I must mention that, like the singers, the musicians wanted the experience and familiarity of playing standard opera repertoire for their future work—something they were not getting nearly enough of in their schools and conservatories. And so, for 45 years, we provided a training ground not only for singers, directors, and conductors, but also for instrumentalists, who went on with their careers into professional orchestras and opera companies.

I was fortunate to have some wonderful musicians working with the company. Hundreds of pianists played for me over the years, all eager to involve themselves in opera. I can't list them all, but I must mention at least two of the artistic, inspiring colleagues at the keyboard I had during the last seasons at the Bowery —Regina Yakubtsiner and Pei-wen Chen. Both of these lovely ladies eagerly awaited their marked scores for the coming new productions in preparation for their rehearsals. Their playing, phrasing, and interpretation of my conducting gestures, for me, was a love affair, since it is such a wonderful and intimate interplay that a conductor can have with musicians who are "in tune" with his musical intentions. What a joy for me when either Regina or Pei-wen was at the keyboard!

***

Looking at the overall picture, when it comes to finalizing any decisions about problems that might arise in the course of a production, I believe it is the orchestra conductor who should have the definitive word, because it is the conductor who must coordinate all the intricacies of the orchestration and all the singing parts, making sure that the meaning of the lyrics is conveyed, providing a good, clean beat, and maintaining an alert left hand to keep all the singers on stage under control. It is the left hand that controls what's going on. It gives intricate cues and shadings and cutoffs, while the right hand is keeping the beat for the orchestra. If the ensemble gets out of hand and starts to rush, it is the left hand that gives the 'stop' and 'go' commands. This requires a coordination that takes many years of working on the same opera to achieve. I considered it a supreme compliment when, in my early conducting years, the musicians would say "Tony has a great left hand!"

Controlling all the onstage and orchestra pit action can only be achieved by conveying a feeling that you are there to help. A metronome won't do it. And the conductor always has to remember to be present and aware of everything that is going on. Opera is no place to be lost in one's own world. The focus must always be directed to all the many people who need to be kept together in one coherent whole. Only when all the pieces are in control can the conductor indulge in his own world and enjoy what he is achieving.

In addition, the conductor must be equipped to discuss how to fix stage positions and actions of the soloists and chorus if they sometimes interfere with the music. On this subject, I must mention how I found it mind-boggling that young conductors who participated in the theatre often didn't take the initiative to learn where soloists and chorus members were to be found on stage during different sections of the ensembles. The result was that when they had to cue a certain singer, their gestures would often be to the wrong person.

Once the singers, orchestra, stage staff, and conductor all see a unified picture together and know their business, there will be a working relationship of excitement, respect, and creativity. And when the final curtain on that production comes down with the audience still cheering, demanding more curtain calls, and the cast embracing and congratulating each other, what a great feeling of satisfaction comes over you!

***

Looking back over my long life in opera, I feel I've succeeded in accomplishing what I set out to do—although there were twists and turns along the way.

I always knew I wanted to be a singer and a teacher. When I was young, I wanted to sing at the Metropolitan Opera, but I've never ever regretted that my life took a different turn. I am confident that I would have been hired at the Met to sing character roles, since good comprimario singers were very much in demand during the war and in the post-World War II days. However, although I was very ambitious in my younger years to sing leading roles, I learned early on that a career as a lead singer didn't suit me. Another thing that stood in my way was my deeply-entrenched work ethic and the assurance I was making a living. I have always been self-supporting and never had a sponsor to help me in my career. Maybe it could be called stubborn pride, but I always felt the need to be independent and provide for myself and the ones I loved.

Even though I didn't have the good fortune to have a sponsor, my family always admired what I did and encouraged me to continue my singing and my studies, even back in my childhood days. Despite the early end of my schooling and my lack of educational degrees, my parents and brothers always let me know how proud they were of me for creating a good life for myself. My brothers kidded me, all in fun, calling me "Maestro Facchino" ("Maestro Laborer"), because I had started out as a butcher and by helping my father in his various restaurant enterprises.

For the readers of this book: Goodbye—opera style! Taking a curtain call on the last Saturday night performance at the Bowery theatre with Rochelle Mancini (Countess) and Gerald Kronberg (Count).

Now that I come to the end of my memoir, I return to something I say so often in this book. There would have been no Amato Opera without my wife Sally. Whether it was with her inspired performances, her beautiful smile when times were hard, with her genius at the sewing machine when we needed a miracle in the costume department, or when she would bring me back to earth when my dreams threatened to be more than reality could bear, she was always there for me and for the Amato Opera family that loved her almost as much as I did.

And, finally, in closing, I can't help but think with immense gratitude of the literally thousands of singers, musicians, pianists, conductors, stage managers, costume designers, and more who have passed through the Amato Opera over the 61 years that we continued to present operas to the public. Sometimes I wake up in the middle of the night and think, "Remember such-and-such a person," and then it leads to another and another. While I can't name all the wonderful people who have helped found and sustain the Amato Opera, believe me, they are all in my thoughts. I think of every single one of them and would like them to know that they are the ones who have made my life such a rich and happy adventure.

—Tony Amato, July, 2010

Appendix 1

ON July 21, 2010, I reached my 90th birthday, which I was happy to celebrate with a number of family and friends. My brother Albert, who is 93, and his wife Zallee came from New London to join me that day, and we all had a very good time eating good food, drinking wine, laughing, telling stories, and—of course—singing together.

One of the highlights for me was when two people read original poems they had written for the occasion. Both refer to events I have written about in this memoir. I reproduce them here for those who might enjoy reading them.

The first is by Rineke Akkerhuis, my dear friend and Amato Opera's last costume designer. The second poem is by Richard Cerullo, the man whose designs for our Amato Opera productions have consistently received wonderful reviews in the press. For almost 40 years, we have worked together, and I truly value his artistry and his friendship.

> When I called "The Amato" to volunteer,
> The answer was: Call back in two weeks, my dear.
> Our theatre undergoes some repairs,
> At the moment we do not have stairs.
>
> Then I called later to set up a meet,
> And the first thing we did was sit down and eat.
> So, over pasta and sauce we had a nice chat,
> Something I'll never regret, or ever forget.
>
> It turned out to change many things for me,
> Since opera was not really my cup of tea.
> It must have hurt you when I made this confession,

but you turned it around, by sharing your passion.
No knowledge of opera, but able to sew,
You said I would pick up the rest on the go.
I had my doubts, but you were so sure,
Do try it till Christmas, that was the lure.
By that time I was getting my bearings
And you had me hooked like a herring.

The dramas ON stage were under your command,
The dramas BACKstage were not so much planned.
You taught me some tricks so I could survive,
And they are as useful in every day life.

How many times have you said:
Always anticipate, think always ahead;
One hand washes the other; Never waste time;
You can spend the penny, but save me the dime.

Watching rehearsal was the best show,
Seeing your passion, your patience, until you explode . . .
     "For the dickens, show me you're an actress,
Don't lay there like an old mattress!"
     "And you, your acting is more like dead wood,
Please paint me the picture . . . Attaboy . . . good, good!"

Getting the best out of people is no easy task,
Getting the details, almost too much to ask.
And checking the props and the pit and the lights,
Checking the house and the lobby for mice,
Checking the singers and checking the checks,
Feeding the chorus after breaking their backs.

Maestro Amato, dear boss and good friend,
This poem has come to its end.
Leaving me one more thing to say:
Happy Happy 90th Birthday.

—Rineke Akkerhuis

When Tony Met Sally

When Tony met Sally
He found the perfect mate
To start their own theatre
In Nineteen Forty-Eight.

Through work and devotion
This visionary team
Were proudly determined
To realize their dream.

An intimate opera
The smallest house in town
Would soon become famous
And bring them great renown.

At 319 Bowery
The stage and lights were set
And Lower Manhattan
Could boast a Mini-Met.

The theater resounded
From Labor Day through May
with Mozart and Verdi,
Puccini, and Bizet.

The countless rehearsals
The shows from year to year
Brought magical memories
For everybody here.

For sixty-one seasons
Through stamina and drive
A genius named Tony
Made opera bloom and thrive.

That team named Amato
Fulfilled what they had planned
They proved by their motto
That Small could be <u>So</u> Grand!
Happy Birthday Tony!

—Richard Cerullo

Appendix 2
Amato Opera Schedule: 1948-2009

(CAPITAL LETTERS INDICATE A NEW PRODUCTION;
(* indicates a revival or a revised production)

1948-1949
Our Lady of Pompeii Church
THE BARBER OF SEVILLE
CAVALLERIA RUSTICANA &
  I PAGLIACCI
DON PASQUALE
LA TRAVIATA

1949-1950
Our Lady of Pompeii Church
AIDA
RIGOLETTO
Don Pasquale
CARMEN
Washington Irving High School
Mozart Festival
THE MARRIAGE OF
FIGARO
THE MAGIC FLUTE
DON GIOVANNI
LA FINTA GIARDINIERA

1950-1951
La Traviata
Aida
Rigoletto
Bleeker Street Theatre Opens
IL TROVATORE
The Barber of Seville
Cavalleria Rusticana & I Pagliacci
Carmen

1951-1952
La Traviata
Aida
FAUST
The Barber of Seville
The Marriage of Figaro
Carmen
The Magic Flute
Don Giovanni
Rigoletto
LA BOHEME

Cavalleria Rusticana & I Pagliacci
Don Pasquale
LA FORZA DEL DESTINO

1952-1953
Aida
The Marriage of Figaro
La Boheme
Carmen
Faust
Il Trovatore
La Traviata
Cavalleria Rusticana & I Pagliacci
Rigoletto
Don Giovanni

1953-1954
Il Trovatore
Aida
The Marriage of Figaro
La Boheme
Carmen
Faust
ZANETTO & I Pagliacci

1954-1955
La Traviata
Faust
The Barber of Seville
Don Pasquale
LUCIA DI LAMMERMOOR
La Boheme
Cavalleria Rusticana & I Pagliacci
Carmen
Don Giovanni

1955-1956
La Boheme
Don Giovanni
Cavalleria Rusticana & I Pagliacci
La Forza del Destino
Rigoletto
La Traviata

Il Trovatore
Don Pasquale
MANON
Aida

1956-1957
TOSCA
Lucia di Lammermoor
The Marriage of Figaro
Faust
Cavalleria Rusticana & I Pagliacci
La Traviata
La Boheme
Don Giovanni
Carmen
The Barber of Seville
Rigoletto
The Magic Flute

1957-1958
La Forza del Destino
La Boheme   *Una arrived*
Rigoletto
Manon   *and sang*
Tosca
Il Trovatore   *in the chorus*
The Magic Flute
The Barber of Seville
Faust
Aida
La Traviata
DIE FLEDERMAUS
Don Giovanni
Carmen
Cavalleria Rusticana & I Pagliacci

1958-1959
Die Fledermaus
The Barber of Seville
Faust
La Boheme
La Traviata
Il Trovatore
Rigoletto
Tosca

1959-1960
Don Giovanni   *Una - Donna Elvira*
Cavalleria Rusticana & I Pagliacci
Carmen
La Boheme
The Magic Flute

Bleeker Street Theatre closes

1960-1961
Professional Company
Rigoletto   *Una - Countess Ceprano*
MADAMA BUTTERFLY
La Traviata
UN GIORNO DI REGNO
LUISA MILLER   *Mermaid small*
                opera workshops
1961-1962   *and Una sang*
Luisa Miller   *lots of roles*
Un Giorno di Regno
AROLDO
La Boheme
Madama Butterfly

1962-1963`
The Barber of Seville
Rigoletto
Madama Butterfly
Luisa Miller
LAND OF SMILES
Carmen

1963-1964
Luisa Miller
Rigoletto
Madama Butterfly

1964-1965
Bowery Theatre Opens
La Boheme
Die Fledermaus
The Marriage of Figaro
La Traviata
HANSEL & GRETEL
Madama Butterfly
Aida
The Barber of Seville
Luisa Miller
The Magic Flute

1965-1966
Tosca
La Boheme
THE PIED PIPER
The Barber of Seville
Madama Butterfly
Il Trovatore
COSI FAN TUTTE

1966-1967
Carmen
Manon
Don Pasquale

Aida
Rigoletto
The Marriage of Figaro
La Boheme
Die Fledermaus
UN BALLO IN MASCHERA
Madama Butterfly
The Pied Piper

1967-1968

The Magic Flute
La Boheme
Don Giovanni
Tosca
Faust
The Barber of Seville
Carmen
La Traviata
Il Trovatore

1968-1969

Madama Butterfly
The Marriage of Figaro
Un Ballo in Maschera
The Magic Flute
La Boheme
Cosi fan tutte
Cavalleria Rusticana & I Pagliacci
Die Fledermaus
Rigoletto
Carmen

1969-1970

Don Giovanni
Tosca
Manon
Die Fledermaus
Aida
Madama Butterfly
La Forza del Destino
La Boheme

1970-1971

La Traviata
The Marriage of Figaro
Faust
La Boheme
Il Trovatore
The Barber of Seville
Carmen
Rigoletto

1971-1972

Aida

Madama Butterfly
The Barber of Seville
The Magic Flute
ANDREA CHENIER
Lucia di Lammermoor
La Boheme
Un Ballo in Maschera

1972-1973 - 25TH ANNIVERSARY

Cosi fan tutte
Tosca
*La Traviata
Die Fledermaus
Don Pasquale
Cavalleria Rusticana & I Pagliacci
The Marriage of Figaro
*Manon

1973-1974

Andrea Chenier
Don Giovanni
La Boheme
FALSTAFF
Madama Butterfly
Carmen

1974-1975

Falstaff
Tosca
Magic Flute
TALES OF HOFFMANN
Rigoletto
Aida

1975-1976

Il Trovatore
La Boheme
Die Fledermaus
LA BATTAGLIA DI LEGNANO
The Marriage of Figaro
Tales of Hoffmann

1976-1977

Don Giovanni
Faust
The Barber of Seville
Falstaff
Madama Butterfly
La Traviata

1977-1978

Cavalleria Rusticana & I Pagliacci
La Boheme
OBERTO

Lucia di Lammermoor
Carmen
Cosi fan tutte

1978-1979
La Traviata
The Magic Flute
Falstaff
LA CENA DELLE BEFFE
The Marriage of Figaro
Tosca

1979-1980
Madama Butterfly
Un Ballo in Maschera
Die Fledermaus
Rigoletto
CRISPINO E LA COMARE
Con Giovanni

1980-1981
Crispino e la Comare
La Boheme
The Barber of Seville
*Aida
Il Trovatore
Manon
La Cena delle Beffe

1981-1982
La Forza del Destino
The Magic Flute
Crispino e la Comare
Andrea Chenier
*Cosi fan tutte
HIN UND ZURUCK & MAVRA
La Traviata
BASTIEN ET BASTIENNE &
    THE IMPRESSARIO

1982-1983 - 35TH ANNIVERSARY
NERONE
Don Giovanni
Carmen
La Boheme
The Marriage of Figaro
Madama Butterfly

1983-1984
Nerone
Aida
*Die Fledermaus
Cavalleria Rusticana & I Pagliacci
La Traviata

Falstaff
IL CAMPANELLO DI NOTTE

1984-1985
VERDI & ALZIRA: VOLTAIRE &
LES AMERICAINS (Drama)
Faust
Tosca
Magic Flute
Cavalleria Rusticana & I Pagliacci
THERESE

1985-1986
Tales of Hoffmann
Il Trovatore
*The Marriage of Figaro
La Boheme
Lucia di Lammermoor
LA SERVA PADRONA
DR. MIRACLE

1986-1987
SALVATOR ROSA
Don Giovanni
Carmen
DR. MIRACLE
Die Fledermaus
Madama Butterfly

1987-1988
Salvator Rosa
La Traviata
La Boheme
Rigoletto
*The Magic Flute

1988-1989
LO SCHIAVO
The Magic Flute
Madama Butterfly
Falstaff
The Marriage of Figaro
Cavalleria Rusticana & I Pagliacci

1989-1990
Don Giovanni
Il Trovatore
The Barber of Seville
Un Ballo in Maschera
La Boheme

1990-1991
Aida
Cosi fan tutte

Die Fledermaus
I DUE FOSCARI
Tosca
La Traviata

1991-1992
The Marriage of Figaro
Carmen
La Boheme
La Forza del Destino
The Magic Flute
THE EMPTY BOTTLE
Cavalleria Rusticana & I Pagliacci

1992-1993
*La Finta Giardiniera
Rigoletto
Faust
The Barber of Seville
Don Giovanni
OTELLO
PROFECIAS

1993-1994
Madama Butterfly
Aida
Die Fledermaus
SUOR ANGELICA
*Cavalleria Rusticana & I Pagliacci
Falstaff

1994-1995
La Boheme
Il Trovatore
La Traviata
Andrea Chenier
The Marriage of Figaro
BLUEBEARD'S CASTLE

1995-1996
*Tosca
Don Giovanni
Madama Butterfly
Don Pasquale
Un Ballo in Maschera

1996-1997
Lucia di Lammermoor
FOSCA
La Boheme
Cosi fan tutte
The Barber of Seville
THE MERRY WIDOW

1997-1998 - GOLDEN ANNIVERSARY
Falstaff
Aida
SECRET OF SUSANNAH
Die Fledermaus
Rigoletto
Tosca
RUDDIGORE

1998-1999
La Boheme
L'AMICO FRITZ & I Pagliacci
THE BOOR
The Barber of Seville
The Magic Flute
The Merry Widow

1999-2000
La Traviata
Carmen
Die Fledermaus
*Manon
Madama Butterfly
Marriage of Figaro

2000-2001
Lucia di Lammermoor
Il Trovatore
La Boheme
*Faust
Don Giovanni
Falstaff

2001-2002
Aida
Tosca
Magic Flute
L'ELISIR D'AMORE
Rigoletto
Carmen

2002 -2003
Madama Butterfly
Cavalleria Rusticana & I Pagliacci
Barber of Seville
Cosi fan tutte
La Traviata
Andrea Chenier

2003-2004
La Boheme
Il Trovatore
Die Fledermaus

The Tales of Hoffmann
The Marriage of Figaro
Lucia di Lammermoor

2004-2005

Magic Flute
Ballo in Maschera
La Boheme
*The Merry Widow
Carmen
L'Elisir d'Amore

2005-2006

Tosca
La Traviata
The Merry Widow
Aida
Don Giovanni
*Faust
THE FOREST

2006-2007

Marriage of Figaro
Rigoletto
Die Fledermaus
*La Forza del Destino
Madama Butterfly
Falstaff

2007-2008

Barber of Seville
Cavalleria Rusticana & I Pagliacci
La Boheme
Don Pasquale
Il Trovatore
Cosi fan tutte

2008-2009

Cosi fan tutte
La Traviata
The Merry Widow
La Boheme
Marriage of Figaro

Bowery Street Theatre closes

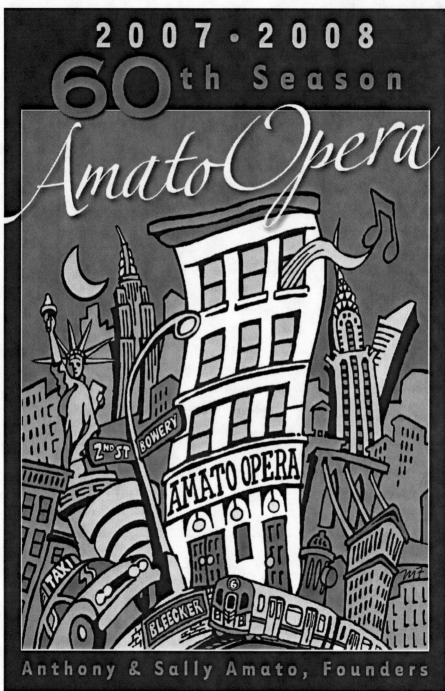

Cover: Mark Freiman

Photo: Harald Schrader

CPSIA information can be obtained at www.ICGtesting.com
Printed in the USA
LVOW040453280911

248205LV00002B/61/P